The Bible without Illusions

THE BIBLE
WITHOUT ILLUSIONS

A. T. and R. P. C. Hanson

SCM PRESS
London

TRINITY PRESS INTERNATIONAL
Philadelphia

First published 1989

SCM Press
26–30 Tottenham Road
London N1 4BZ

Trinity Press International
3725 Chestnut Street
Philadelphia, Pa. 19104

British Library Cataloguing in Publication Data

Hanson, Anthony, 1916-
  The Bible without illusions.
  I. Title   II. Hanson, R. P. C. (Richard Patrick
  Crosland, 1916–88)
  220.6
  ISBN 0–334–00101–3

Library of Congress Cataloging-in-Publication Data

Hanson, Antony Tyrrell.
  The Bible without illusions / A.T. and R.P.C. Hanson.
      p.   cm.
  Includes bibliographical references.
  ISBN 0–334–00101–3
  1. Bible—Study.   2.Bible—Criticism, interpretation, etc.
  3. Bible—Hermeneutics.   I. Hanson, R. P. C. (Richard Patrick
  Crosland), 1916–   II. Title.
  BS600.2.H357   1989
  220.1—dc20

Typeset at The Spartan Press Ltd, Lymington, Hants
and printed in Great Britain by
Richard Clay Ltd, Bungay, Suffolk

In grateful memory of our schoolmasters,
who taught us to love the Bible,
but not to idolize it.

Contents

Preface

Before the disease which brought my late brother to the grave within the space of five months had declared itself, we had virtually completed the manuscript of this book. It is therefore to be regarded as being quite as much our joint work as are the other two books which we have written together, *Reasonable Belief* (1980) and *The Identity of the Church* (1987).

I wish to express my gratitude to my wife and to Mrs Diana Mills of Knayton for invaluable help in reading the proofs.

A.T.H.

Chapter One

The Study of the Bible Today

One often hears the demand, made by ministers and laity alike, that those who are training for the ordained ministry should not be burdened with too much academic study of the Bible, but that their curriculum should include 'the ability to apply the scriptures to the needs of the world', to quote a recent speaker. This sounds good. But on examination it turns out to be a remarkably simplistic suggestion. How does anyone apply the scriptures to the needs of the world? Are we to teach our prospective clergy that at all costs they are not to suffer witches to live, that in view of the present distress it is better that nobody should marry, that there is no future life, that women must be kept out of public life and confined to the church, the crêche and the kitchen, that slaves should obey their masters, that the guilt of the death of Christ is attached to every succeeding generation of Jews since the crucifixion? We shall find all these views endorsed at various parts of the scriptures. Are we to teach them that God is pure, unqualified love, and also that he is angry with sinners, that Jesus propitiated God's wrath so that he was able to forgive us, and also that God's love takes the initiative and reaches us even while we are sinners, that Jesus apparently disavowed divinity in St Mark's Gospel and eagerly claimed it in St John's, that Matthew and Luke say that Jesus rejected the temptation to perform spectacular miracles in order to win disciples during his temptation in the wilderness, and that according to St John's Gospel a few weeks later he turned a large quantity of water into wine in order to oblige some friends at a wedding? All these beliefs, at least implicitly, can be found in the New Testament. How do we apply the Sermon on the Mount to the problem of nuclear weapons, the threat to the environment, drug taking and the practice of abortion, and the prevalence of terrorism? To take one apparently simple subject only, that of divorce: in St Mark's Gospel Jesus absolutely rules out any form of divorce; in St

Matthew's Gospel he allows an exception – 'except for the case of adultery'. Either therefore Jesus did not pronounce that marriage was indissoluble, because he permitted it to be ended in the case of adultery, (whatever he meant by 'adultery') or the church at a very early period indeed permitted itself to modify his rigorous pronouncement by making an exception in the case of divorce. Which is correct? What conclusions are we to draw? What is the simple straightforward teaching upon this subject?

Applying the scriptures to the needs of the world is manifestly then a complex, delicate, exacting discipline, not at all a matter of drawing simple, obvious conclusions from a plain and easily comprehensible text. And in addition, it is naive to imagine that we can ignore the long and tangled history of Christian doctrine which is in fact the record of how Christians from the earliest times have attempted to apply the scriptures to the needs of the world, from Ignatius of Antioch to Karl Barth. That history has made the Christianity which we now profess, the tradition in which we stand. We cannot leap directly from the scriptures to the present day as if the history of Christian doctrine had never happened.

It is, however, becoming increasingly difficult for those who are training for the ordained ministry to find the time to devote to serious study of the Bible. This is because so many other subjects are now making claims to a place on the ordinands' curriculum, the formation of the spiritual life; preparation for pastoral ministry; learning about other religions; theology, systematic or historical; church history; and most recently a large contribution from that ambiguous territory the social sciences, in the form of a study of human relations, managerial skills, and similar topics. Six years would hardly suffice to cover this ground adequately. Three years is grossly insufficient; two years a mere farce.

Beyond the theological college today everywhere laity are being enrolled in courses and groups to study the Bible. Bible study is often held up as the universal panacea for the ills of the church. But in the vast majority of cases this Bible study is study without tears, or a study of the Bible which carefully steers round, omits or plays down all the difficulties and all the problems. It is a study conducted in an atmosphere of illusion. And when men and women finally emerge from the theological colleges and are ordained, all that the great majority of them can do, whether they are preaching, teaching or taking part in Bible study, is to take refuge in one illusion or another. Either they lapse into fundamentalism or a conservatism which is really a kind of unacknowledged fundamentalism; or they adopt a kind of biblical pragmatism, using those bits of the Bible which they find congenial and ignoring everything else. Consequently, outside the Roman Catholic Church, where there has been a revival of biblical preaching, the level of preaching and teaching has reached a low point. It would not be unfair to say that the average church-goer does not expect to be taught anything from the sermons he hears. He expects to be bored by the sermon.

This book has been written under the conviction that the interpretation of the Bible needs entire seriousness and scrupulous honesty. It is indeed the dishonesty of much contemporary treatment of the Bible that has largely impelled the authors to write it. The work is not a 'debunking' of the Bible, but an attempt to show what qualities and what preliminary assumptions are needed in order that the Bible shall be genuinely understood and genuinely interpreted. The book is concerned to make it clear that honest scholarship and honest interpretation must acknowledge that a revolution has taken place in the understanding of the Bible during the last two hundred years and that to try to deny or play down or disguise the results of this revolution is to be faithful to neither God nor man. Opponents of what is widely called a 'liberal' approach to the Bible often write as if those who accept the results of biblical criticism were wantonly playing about with dangerous and upsetting ideas in order to annoy and disturb the faithful. But this is far from the truth, and for anyone to assume this is to reveal how little he or she understands the nature of biblical criticism. The techniques and assumptions of contemporary biblical criticism are not optional whims nor *jeux d'esprit* which can be taken up or left alone. They are the tools and presuppositions of a genuine, methodical, scholarly discipline which is for the use of experts, and those who refuse to accept them show that they are simply incompetent in this field of exploring the biblical literature. This state of affairs may be lamented (though we do not think that it is in fact lamentable), but it cannot be denied or rejected without ineptitude. We adopt the discipline (we only refrain from calling it science because the word is so ambiguous) of biblical criticism because we must if we are to be honest. And we recognize the great changes which it has made in our understanding of the Bible because for honest men and women there is no alternative.

We are well aware that our insistence on the necessity of accepting the full implications of biblical criticism can pose problems for many

perfectly reasonable Christians who are far from being fundamentalists and are quite ready to listen to any competent scholar on the
subject of the Bible. But they have certain misgivings. Let us try to
voice these misgivings, for there is no doubt just such a person exists
inside each one of us. We shall pick out three questions.

1. 'If we pursue the critical study of the Bible to its logical
conclusions, we shall be compelled to deny, or at least radically
modify, accepted dogmas of the church.'

This is a misgiving which particularly afflicts members of the
'catholic' wing of the church. It is by no means confined to unin-
formed lay people, but affects the most learned scholars also. A good
example is A. Feuillet, a distinguished French Roman Catholic New
Testament scholar. In a long article written in defence of the
completely historical nature of the Fourth Gospel, he begins by
pointing out that the Second Vatican Council laid it down that the
four gospels were historical documents and that they faithfully
recorded what Jesus really did and really taught. Later on he writes
as follows:

> If we suppose that the Gospel of John is not that which without
> any doubt it claims to be, a valuable historical witness to Jesus, we
> must then conclude that the entire Church, from its origins until
> the end of the nineteenth century or the beginning of the twen-
> tieth century (we could very well say until the advent of modern
> scientific exegesis), that all the Fathers and all the Doctors of the
> Church, all the great theologians, all the Councils and all the
> mystics were grossly mistaken on the subject of this Gospel
> because they unanimously believed in the reality of the events and
> of the discourses of Jesus which John relates to us.

And he goes on to point out that if we once admit that the Johannine
Gospel is not solidly historical we shall be deprived of the biblical
witness to the most basic teachings of the Catholic Church, the
mysteries of the Trinity and the incarnation, and the mystery of the
Virgin Mary, Mother of the Church.*

Now this is an exaggerated account of the position, written by a
scholar who is alarmed at the direction in which some of his colleagues
are moving. If we deny the full historical nature of the Fourth Gospel

*See an article, 'Réflexions sur quelques versets de Jn. 6. et sur le Réalisme historique
du Quatrième Évangile' in *Divinitas* 1986 (1), 30, pp. 5, 50, our own translation.

we do not need to jettison the doctrines of the incarnation, nor of the Trinity, though we certainly need to modify the way in which we express them. Nor do we need to say that all the Fathers, doctors, Councils and mystics were so grossly mistaken about the Fourth Gospel as to render their writings worthless to us. But by and large if we are honest we must accept the conclusion of the majority of the most competent experts on the Fourth Gospel, which is that this Gospel is not a straightforward history of Jesus, and that it conveys to us Jesus' teaching only in a very much modified form. If we take Feuillet's alternative, which is to assume that the Fourth Gospel must be reliable history because the church authorities (in this case Vatican II) say so, we shall find ourselves holding beliefs that are based on legend or purely traditional belief. It is not enough to say 'we believe it because the church has always believed it'. Intellectual honesty requires that we give more solid reasons for our belief.

2. 'Well, let us accept a moderate dose of biblical criticism. We are not fundamentalists. But we will drop it when it begins to hurt us.'

This is an attitude which is very common among clergy of all traditions. Most of them will have been taught the elements of biblical and historical criticism during their period of training. But many of them will never really have accepted it, and step easily into a sort of quasi-fundamentalism when it comes to preaching and teaching. Two examples may be quoted, one relating to that Fourth Gospel which is such a bone of contention for many Christians today. Some years ago a very distinguished minister of the Church of Scotland, a much sought-after preacher, and a real man of God, was delivering a sermon to a large group of Church of England clergy at a conference devoted to the art of preaching. He took as his subject the account of Nicodemus' visit to Jesus by night as related in John 3. He gave a vivid description of Nicodemus stealing out by night: 'The clouds', he said, 'were scudding across the moon.' Nicodemus made his way stealthily to visit this new rabbi; and there followed a moving exhortation to be open to the Spirit, as Nicodemus was urged to be by Jesus in this discourse. Splendid and effective! But if you believe that this discourse was largely composed by John in order to show the difference that Christianity made to traditional Jewish belief, and that it does not accurately reproduce the words of Jesus – well, you will not be inclined to treat the narrative in John 3 in this manner. You will not reject the passage as irrelevant to Christian faith, but you will adopt a different approach. This distinguished Scottish preacher was certainly not a fundamentalist, and if challenged he would undoubtedly have said that we must accept reasonable biblical criticism. But he obviously had not considered it necessary before composing his sermon to pay any attention to what the experts were saying about the historicity of the Fourth Gospel.

This attitude sometimes results in a sort of fideism: 'I will believe it because I want to believe it, whatever the historical evidence.' Some time ago a New Testament scholar was giving a lecture on the origins of the Christian ordained ministry and pointing out that there is no solid evidence for the traditional doctrine of the apostolic succession, i.e. the claim that the authority of the modern episcopate can be shown to have been handed down by succession from Jesus to the apostles and by them to the first bishops and so to us today. A member of the audience, an Anglican priest, was shocked by the conclusion and exclaimed: 'Well, I shall go on believing in the apostolic succession, whatever the evidence.' He is, of course, entitled to do this, as long as he is willing to be classed with the followers of any lunatic supposition you may choose. If you believe something in the teeth of the evidence just because you want to believe it, you have disqualified yourself to reason with educated people. You have left yourself with no defence against the accusation of outright superstition.

3. 'The conclusions of the biblical critics are entirely subjective. What one competent critic will accept as true, another will deny as legend.'

Here undoubtedly the opponents of biblical criticism have a strong argument. When we first begin to study the biblical experts in any depth this is certainly the impression we receive. This is particularly the case with regard to the synoptic gospels. The critics have not succeeded in producing any clear set of criteria which would enable us to decide, for example, how much of Jesus' teaching recorded in the first three gospels really goes back to Jesus and how much is the contribution of the early church. But this does not mean that we can wash our hands of biblical criticism. There are certain conclusions that stand out, certain basic assumptions which must considerably modify how we use the Bible. Here are a few taken very much at random. Many more could be added.

(*a*) Everything narrated in the Old Testament about the history of Israel up till the entry into Canaan is either myth or legend. Solid history only begins after the entry, and even then there is a considerable element of legend.

(*b*) Mark is the earliest of the four gospels and was used by both 'Matthew' and Luke in the composition of their gospels.

(*c*) The Fourth Gospel does not give us a picture of Jesus as he actually appeared in history.

(*d*) Paul did not write the Pastoral Epistles (I and II Timothy and Titus). They probably belong to the early years of the second century. It can safely be claimed that the best scholars in all Christian traditions would accept these conclusions.

It is true indeed that the subjective nature of the technique of biblical criticism is something which it is hard for the church to accept. We would much rather have clear definite conclusions on all important questions concerning the Bible. But God has not willed that it should be so. He has chosen rather that we should live in a period of uncertainty, when many traditional beliefs must be modified or abandoned, and much reconstructing (*perestroika?*) of the Christian faith must be undertaken. We can console ourselves with the thought that this is not the first time in the history of the church that this has happened. We can point to several other such periods. From about AD 150 till 300 it must have been very difficult for Christian intellectuals to choose between what was later regarded as orthodoxy and the claims of the various forms of Christian Gnosticism that were available. During almost the whole of the fourth century Christian thinkers in the East must have been perplexed at the challenge to the Christian doctrine of God presented by Arianism. There was no authoritative centre of orthodoxy to which they could appeal. Much later, during the twelfth century in Western Europe we know that much intellectual turmoil was caused by the influx of Aristotelianism from the Arabs via the Jews. Eventually in the thirteenth century the issue was largely solved by the massive genius of Thomas Aquinas. But Christians could not know that this was to happen and Thomas' own teachings were denounced by the Archbishop of Paris soon after his death. Then came the Renaissance with its accession of new knowledge, and the beginning of the rise of modern science from the early fourteenth century onwards. All this the church had to endure. We may be sure that thinking Christians during those various epochs were just as much perplexed about what to believe as we are, and we may be sure that then as now there were plenty of people ready to denounce the new learning or the new orthodoxy and to assure their fellow Christians that these new ideas would only bring trouble and lack of faith. But God brought his church through these periods of doubt. We can be confident that he will bring us safely through also if we trust him and remain faithful to what appears to us to be the truth.

Chapter Two

The Facts about the Bible

Since we are intending in this book to explain what the Bible is and how it should be used, it may be as well to begin by giving a brief account of the Bible as an ancient document, or rather a collection of ancient documents.

We must then describe the Bible as a collection of ancient documents that have in common the fact that they are regarded by the Christian church as their holy book, their scriptures, akin to the Vedas, the Upanishads, the Mahabharata, and the Puranas of the Hindus, the Tripitaka of the Buddhists, and the Quran of the Muslims. This collection of documents was written at a great variety of times. Its contents come from as far back as 1,000 BC (Song of Deborah in Judges 5 perhaps) and as recently as about AD 120 (Second Epistle of Peter probably). The documents comprising the Old Testament cover a far wider time-scale (1000 BC till 165 BC) than do those of the New. All the New Testament documents were written within a period of seventy years (roughly AD 50 till AD 120). The Old Testament by itself is the Bible of Judaism, which Jews do not of course call the Old Testament. Their name for it is either 'The Bible' or 'The Hebrew Scriptures' or 'The Tenak' (an acronym for *Torah* (Law), *Nebi'im* (Prophets) and *Kethubim* (the Writings)).

These writings were originally composed in three different languages: the vast majority of the Old Testament was written in Hebrew. Hebrew was the common language of the Jews till the return from Babylonian exile about 522 BC. By that time Hebrew had dropped out of common use. Ordinary people spoke Aramaic, which at that time was the *lingua franca* of the near east. Hebrew remained in use as a sacred language. Aramaic is a language about as closely related to Hebrew as Italian is to French. Consequently we find some parts of the latest books in the Old Testament written in

Aramaic; i.e. Daniel 2.4 – 7.28; some parts of the Book of Ezra, and one verse in Jeremiah (Jer. 10.11). The New Testament is entirely written in what is called Koinē Greek, that is the Greek that was spoken as the *lingua franca* of the eastern Roman Empire during the first century of the Christian era.

However, these sacred texts were translated into other languages and the earliest translations have been very influential in the exposition and transmission of the contents of the Bible. Some time between 250 BC and the birth of Jesus the entire Old Testament was translated into Greek. This is usually called the Septuagint (LXX for short) because of the legendary account of its origin: it was supposed to have been translated by seventy scholars working together in Egypt, who miraculously all separately produced the same translation. But we now know that there were other Greek translations in use, some of which were known to some of the writers of the New Testament, and also that the LXX is not by a single translator, nor made all at the same time. Naturally, the many quotations from the Old Testament which we meet in the New Testament are in Greek, mostly from the Septuagint version. The New Testament also was soon translated into other languages; among the earliest was the Syriac version, i.e. the translation into the language that was the native tongue of Palestinians in Jesus' time, and indeed of Jesus himself.

Equally important was the translation of the entire Bible into Latin, which was begun perhaps in North Africa by the end of the second century AD. By the year AD 400 at least the Western Church read its Bible in Latin. Few people had access to the Greek and fewer still to the Hebrew. This state of affairs continued throughout the Middle Ages in the West. One of the causes of the Reformation was the rediscovery by Western scholars of the Greek New Testament and the Hebrew Old Testament. The Western Church in the Middle Ages on the whole failed to translate the Bible into the newly emerging languages, that is the Romance languages and the languages of the northern nations, English, German, or the Scandinavian languages, and the Celtic languages on the western fringe of Europe. Consequently most of the earliest translations into these languages date from the sixteenth century or later.

With the missionary expansion of the church into the third world during the nineteenth century, a huge programme of translation was undertaken, much of it under the auspices of the British and Foreign Bible Society and its associated organizations. This is still continuing; we hear every year of a translation of the Bible into a language of Africa or of some other part of the world. Until recently this work was entirely carried out by Protestants, since the Roman Catholic Church maintained the mediaeval disapproval of translating the Bible into the vernacular. Since Vatican II, however, all this has changed, and Roman Catholics co-operate with other Christians in the work of translating the Bible. We in England have been deluged with alternative English translations during the past fifty years, so that we are not likely easily to forget that our English Bibles *are* translations and not the original. In many countries of the third world, there is only one translation. This is commended to what is often a semi-literate Christian reading public. Those who read it have no means of telling how accurate their version is. This must result in some misunderstanding of the Bible, especially in places where a fundamentalist approach to the Bible has been taught.

No absolutely original manuscripts of the Bible have been preserved. We do not have, for example, the original manuscript of the Gospel which Luke wrote, or an autograph letter of Paul. Still less may we expect to come across the original manuscript of any book of the Old Testament. The very earliest texts of the New Testament are papyrus fragments that have been preserved in the sands of Egypt. There is, for example a fragment of the Fourth Gospel which the experts say dates from not later than AD 150. But the earliest complete copies of the entire Bible are not earlier than about AD 300. Codex Vaticanus and Codex Sinaiticus are of the early fourth century; they are two of the most important manuscripts for establishing the original text. But of course both these codices, written on parchment not papyrus, contain the New Testament in Greek and the Old Testament also in Greek, i.e. the Septuagint version. There are hundreds and hundreds of manuscripts of the New Testament, dating from *c*. AD 300 till any time up to the Renaissance. Almost equally important are the many Latin versions of the New Testament, some of which are earlier than some Greek manuscripts. Scholars can also call on the help of early versions in other languages, Syriac (as we have seen), Coptic (the language of Egypt), Old Gothic, Armenian, Georgian, etc. The early church did not have the same inhibitions about translating the scriptures as the mediaevals.

When we ask, what are the earliest surviving manuscripts of the Old Testament, we have a different picture. We are talking now about the Old Testament in Hebrew, not the Septuagint since the mediaeval church on the whole was content to read its scriptures in translation.

Hebrew manuscripts of the Old Testament were preserved only by the jews. Until about fifty years ago, the oldest known manuscript of the Hebrew Bible came from about the ninth century AD. Some centuries earlier Jewish scholars had agreed on a standard text, called the Massoretic Text, and had done their best to see that all alternative texts were destroyed. However, the finds in the desert by the Dead Sea, where the Qumran Community was located, include a very large number of books, or fragments of books, of the Hebrew Bible. So that today we have a Hebrew text of the Old Testament that takes us back almost a thousand years earlier than the previously known earliest Hebrew manuscript. It must be said that on the whole the Qumran text is not very different from the Massoretic text, which suggests that the process of standardization had already begun by the time of the Qumran Community (roughly 200 BC to AD 70). The actual contents of the Septuagint and of the Hebrew Bible differ considerably. But for details of this we refer you to our section on the Canon of Scripture. But even with the assistance of the Qumran finds, the Hebrew manuscripts which we have date from hundreds of years after the composition of most of the Old Testament.

Since we shall be spending the rest of this book in describing the nature and function of the Bible, it is appropriate at this stage to give some indication of what the Bible is not. We mention four mistaken estimates of what the Bible is, not just for the sake of doing so, but because all of them have been believed by some Christians at some period, and indeed all of them are still held by some Christians today.

1. *The Bible is not a theological textbook*

This may seem a surprising assertion, since one naturally associates theology with the Bible, and all Christians claim that the theology they hold is based on the Bible. It is quite true that the Bible is a theological book, in the sense that it contains a great deal of material about God and many of its authors can legitimately be called theologians. But it is not a theological textbook because none of it was written in order to provide the basis for a theology. In fact the various books of the Bible were written with a very wide range of motives. Some of the books are very untheological, even anti-theological, such as Ecclesiastes or even the Book of Job. The Christian church has quite rightly drawn its theology from the Bible, mostly of course from the New Testament. But it has to be *drawn*. It is not there all neatly catalogued ready to be transferred into our primers of theology. This is on the whole the mistake made by the Fathers of the church, as we shall see. They believed that doctrines such as the incarnation and the Trinity, as understood in their days, were already held by all the biblical writers, those of the Old Testament as well as those of the New. But it is not as easy as that: we must indeed seek the sources of our theology in the Bible, and a theology that is not based on the Bible is not Christian. But the Bible as a whole was not intended to teach theology and we err if we treat it as if it was.

2. *Likewise the Bible is not a handbook of Christian worship*

At times in the history of the church some Christians have been led into the belief that it was a handbook of worship. For instance at the Reformation it was plain that one of the features of the church's life that most needed reformation was its worship. The way in which the eucharist was celebrated and utilized had undergone a considerable process of corruption. One great reformed tradition, that stemming from John Calvin (very confusingly called the Reformed or Presbyterian tradition), assumed that the best way of reforming the church's worship was to return to the model of worship to be found in the New Testament. Consequently they abandoned the church's year, the sequence of the mass, the use of a fixed liturgy, and many other minor elements such as liturgical vestments and candles. Unfortunately, however, the New Testament does not give us any detailed information about how Christians worshipped on a Sunday. Only from about AD 150 onwards do we have anything like detailed account of the Christian eucharist. The consequence was that much reformed (and Reformed) worship was very greatly impoverished, and at the worst became a series of sermons interspersed with free prayer and a few hymns. Today it is very widely admitted indeed that the New Testament cannot provide us with a detailed pattern of worship. As far as the eucharist is concerned all the major traditions in the West have reverted to a eucharistic order based on that of the church of the first four centuries.

3. *The Bible is not an accurate account of the origin of the world, nor is it a reliable history of the origin of mankind, nor even of the origin of Israel*

The beliefs here denied have been held by all Christians from the very beginning until about a hundred and fifty years ago. They are still held by a great many Christians. The realization that the Bible is not a scientific textbook first began to dawn on Christians in this country in the last century and has probably been fairly widely accepted by now. Most of us do not regard Adam and Eve as historical characters and do not hold that woman was literally formed out of man's side. But the realization that the story of Israel's origin from Abraham till almost the time of Saul and David is not history but legend can hardly be described as having affected very many Christians even today. We still hear sermons giving a psychological analysis of Abraham's feelings on Mount Moriah, or a vivid account of how the Red Sea dried up at the waving of Moses' rod. This is not to say that those parts of the Bible which are myth or legend are of no value. Very much the reverse. But we can only appreciate their value if we accept them for what they are, and do not pretend that they are something which they are not.

4. *The Bible does not provide information about future history; it is not a divine crossword puzzle; it is not a magic book*

At various times in the church's history the Bible may be said to have been regarded in all these ways. There have been people (and there are still some today) who look in the Bible for detailed prophecies about what is to happen to the world during the next few years. They delude themselves. The writers of the Bible knew nothing about the circumstances of our day; they were not divinely inspired with knowledge about the remote future. We have used the phrase 'a divine crossword puzzle' in order to describe the technique of those who believe that the message of the Bible needs to be decoded, often by the means of numerology. The rabbis who lived during the second, third and fourth centuries of our era were given to this sort of numerology, which they called *gematria*. For example, one rabbinic speculation was based on the word 'gently' in Isaiah 8.6: 'Because this people have refused the waters of Shiloah that flow gently . . .' The Hebrew word for 'gently' here is *le'at*; the rabbi in question, using *gematria*, calculated that the letters of *le'at* add up to forty. But in order to prepare a ritual bath sufficient for lustration purposes, forty *seahs* of water are needed. Therefore the pool of Siloam could be used for ritual lustration. Christians were not immune from this form of exegetical lunacy; the author of the *Epistle of Barnabas*, a Christian work of the AD 120s, proudly points out (9.6) that the number of young men who accompanied Abraham in his expedition to rescue Lot recounted in Genesis was 318 (Gen. 14.14). By his method of *gematria*, based on Greek words, not Hebrew, the name of Jesus adds up to 318.

Therefore the incident described in Genesis 14 was a prophecy of the coming of Christ!

Finally the Bible is not a magic book. There was a custom among some Christians when they were uncertain as to what course they should take in the future, to consult the *sortes biblicae*, the biblical oracle. You opened the Bible at random (after prayer), put your finger down on a verse without looking, and that verse was supposed to give you guidance as to what you ought to do. This is to treat the Bible as a magic book. All three misuses of the Bible detailed under heading (4) may not unfairly be described as superstitious uses of the Bible, a form of superstition to which Protestants were just as prone as Catholics, indeed even more prone than Catholics because they relied more on the Bible.

Chapter Three

The New Testament Interpretation of Scripture

'We base our faith on the word of God and not on the traditions of men.' This watch-word has held an attraction for Christians all down the ages. It is easy to understand why this should be so. In the course of the centuries the original faith of the Christians did become altered, and certainly by the year AD 1500 gross corruptions had crept into both the faith and practice of the church in the West at least. Against the authority of the contemporary church the only authority to which would-be reformers could appeal was the authority of the Bible. When they made this appeal they were told by the church authorities of their day that all the things they objected to had the sanction of tradition. Naturally their cry was: 'The Bible alone and not the tradition of the church!'

The Reformers were not the first to do this. The church Fathers always sought to base their doctrine on scripture and only with the greatest reluctance did they call on the aid of tradition to supplement scripture. The example of the Reformers in appealing to scripture against tradition has been followed by some moderns, from both the conservative and the radical wings of the church. Conservative Christians, almost always in defence of some form of fundamentalism, will often declare that they base their doctrine on the Bible alone and that they repudiate the tradition of the church. For the most part they are not aware of the extent to which the writers of the New Testament were themselves dependent on tradition in their interpretation of the Old Testament. Such conservative Christians will either espouse the Reformers' principle of 'the internal witness of the Holy Spirit' (i.e. the Holy Spirit can be relied on always to tell you whether your interpretation is correct), or they assume without saying so that the Bible is self-interpreting.

But there are scholars belonging to the radical wing who also eagerly repudiate the church's tradition in their exposition of scripture. Anyone, for instance, who has read Martin Werner's book *The Formation of Christian Dogma*★ will be impressed by his condemnation of the way doctrine developed in the second century and his criticism of what he regards as a 'sacramental' tendency in the church of the second generation onwards. In fact Werner is not content to appeal to the New Testament against the tradition of the church. He appeals to Paul against John. He believes that things went disastrously wrong between the writing of the genuine Pauline letters and the composition of the Fourth Gospel.

Werner's thesis, if generally accepted by Christians, would mean the end of Christianity. A New Testament that is so interpreted as to be fatally divided against itself cannot be used as the norm of doctrine. There must be some agreed interpretation of the Bible in the church, no matter how general and unconcerned with details it may be. In fact an entirely uninterpreted Bible has never existed. We proceed to give evidence in defence of this assertion.

II

The essence of our argument lies in the simple statement that the New Testament writers themselves in interpreting scripture (which for them meant what we call the Old Testament) took for granted a strong element of traditional Jewish interpretation. That everyone must approach scripture with some presuppositions is obvious, even if the presuppositions only consist in the reasons why one is sufficiently interested in scripture to read it. But in the case of the New Testament writers we can be much more specific than this. Every one of the writers of the New Testament exhibits some traces of the influence of traditional Jewish interpretation of scripture. For none of them was scripture a *tabula rasa*, a volume about which they had no pre-existing theological convictions. We will confine ourselves to the main authors of the New Testament in illustrating this principle, but it could certainly be proved from any writer of the New Testament whom one might choose to examine.

In the first place we may observe that the very use of the language of scripture must carry some element of interpretation. The New

★Martin Werner, *The Formation of Christian Dogma*, E.T. London 1957.

Testament writers wrote in Greek, and when they quoted scripture they quoted it (almost, but not quite, invariably: see Mark 15.34; Matt. 27.46) in Greek only. But any Greek translation of the original Hebrew was to some extent also an interpretation. The LXX, which was the standard translation in use during the first century, had certain characteristics which made it something much less than an entirely transparent medium for conveying the light of the original. The translators for instance modified extreme examples of anthropomorphism when God was the subject. They tended on the whole to be universalistic and to interpret the Psalms and Isaiah in a sense favourable to Gentiles where possible. Occasionally they modify the Hebrew so as to make it conform to contemporary practice, and so on. The LXX was not indeed the only Greek translation used by New Testament writers. We know that there were others in the field, and it is very probable that they were sometimes used by New Testament writers. But these too would have their interpretative elements. It is also true that some of the authors of the New Testament could go to the Hebrew and translate it for themselves. This is certainly the case with Paul, with the author of the First Gospel, and with St John the Divine (author of the Book of Revelation). But no New Testament writer is entirely independent of some current Greek translation of scripture, and most of them are content to use the LXX or some other version even when they could translate the Hebrew.

Let us now see how contemporary Jewish interpretation of scripture can be detected behind the scriptural exegesis of the New Testament writers. We have no space to give more than one example in each case, but many others could be quoted. Jesus himself, on occasion, shows that he accepts traditional exegesis. A good example is Mark 2.26 (parallels Matt. 12.3; Luke 6.4). Jesus is defending his disciples when they are accused of breaking the sabbath by plucking ears of corn and rubbing them to extract the grain. He cites the example of David in I Samuel 21.1–6. In referring to the incident Jesus takes for granted that David had a band of warriors with him. But if we look it up we find that the band of warriors was an invention of David's. He pretends that he had arranged to meet them and that therefore he needs a lot of bread. The author of I Samuel saw nothing wrong in this, but subsequent exegesis would tend to portray David as an ideal figure and therefore assumed that he was speaking the truth about the young men who, he claimed, were to accompany him. Jesus accepts this piece of traditional exegesis without question.

From many examples which could be cited from Paul we take one, a famous – indeed a notorious – one. In I Corinthians 10.1–11 Paul is drawing a comparison between the situation of the Israelites during the sojourn in the desert and the situation of the contemporary Corinthian church. He compares the rock from which Moses drew the water with Christ (rather, he does more: he identifies it with Christ). In the course of his exegesis he writes: 'They (the Israelites) drank from the supernatural Rock which followed them.' There is nothing in scripture about, the rock following the Israelites, but we know from rabbinic writings of a much later date that there was a tradition to the effect that the rock, not content with supplying water on one occasion, followed them about providing water during the whole period of the desert wanderings. Paul simply takes this piece of traditional interpretation for granted.

It is generally agreed that the author of the First Gospel was well trained in traditional Jewish exegesis. It is probably this that enables him to make a strikingly christological interpretation of a verse in Isaiah. In Matthew 1.23 we find Isaiah 7.14 interpreted as a prophecy of the birth of Jesus from a virgin. In fact the original Hebrew does not use the word 'virgin' at all. Isaiah was referring to a young married woman, not a virgin. But the Greek word *parthenos* does mean 'virgin', and it is probable that already Jewish exegesis had interpreted this text as referring to the Messiah's being born from the virgin Israel. There is a similar usage in the *Hodayoth* (Hymns of the Qumran Community), where the Community among whom the Messiah is soon to be born is described in terms of a woman in travail with a child (*1QH* 3.8–9). Thus traditional Jewish exegesis in this instance helped early Christians to interpret a text from Isaiah in a christological sense.

If we were to read through the whole of the eleventh chapter of the Letter to the Hebrews in the light of the traditional understanding of Israel's history we could no doubt find many places where the author of Hebrews is making use of traditional interpretation. One such is Hebrews 11.27. Moses is described as having left Egypt 'not being afraid of the anger of the king'. In fact in Exodus 2.14–15 he is represented as having been afraid; 'then Moses was afraid, and thought, "Surely the thing (i.e. his having killed the Egyptian) is known". When Pharaoh heard of it, he sought to kill Moses'. But hagiographical tradition could not admit that the great Moses should be afraid of Pharaoh. The Hebrew word for 'he was afraid' is very like the Hebrew word for 'he saw'. Jewish exegetical tradition preferred to translate it: 'And Moses understood and said to himself. . . .' The author of Hebrews takes this interpretation for granted.

The Fourth Gospel is full of scriptural allusions, and it would not be at all difficult to show that many of them are influenced by traditional Jewish exegesis. We will choose one out of many. In John 1.51 Jesus is represented as making this promise to Nathanael: 'you will see the heaven opened and the angels of God ascending and descending upon the Son of Man.' This was an allusion to Jacob's vision of a ladder reaching up to heaven, related in Genesis 28.10–17. Not surprisingly, it was the subject of extensive speculation among the learned in Israel. This was after all a direct vision of heaven. Jacob was privileged to behold the angels of God. Some suggested that there was an ideal image of Jacob in heaven; others that the ladder rested upon Jacob himself. All were agreed that the vision had great significance for an understanding of the relation of the people of Israel to God. When John chose to link this passage with Jesus it is impossible to believe that he was unaware of this traditional speculation: he uses it as a method of setting forth the lofty christology which he expounds in his gospel.

III

The authors of the New Testament, however, are not completely dependent on Jewish exegetical tradition. On the contrary, their interpretation of scripture, though it has its starting point in contemporary Jewish exegesis, diverges from it in the most significant way. Jewish exegesis was centred on the Torah, the law of Moses. Christian exegesis is centred on Christ. The Old Testament is quoted very frequently throughout the New Testament, in the great majority of cases in order to show that the Old Testament was in some way prefiguring Christ. The New Testament writers differ quite considerably in the method they use of finding Christ in scripture, but they are all agreed that Christ is to be found there. One of the earliest elements in the Christian creed was that Jesus died and rose again 'according to the scriptures'. See I Corinthians 15.3–4.

In the first place Jesus must have seen himself as one called to fulfil a *rôle* which had been foretold in scripture. There is much dispute among scholars as to which *rôle* out of a number possible it was that Jesus believed he was called to follow: Son of Man? Servant of the Lord? Messiah? Eschatological prophet? But whichever we choose it will prove to have been defined and described in scripture. We personally hold the view which is accepted by only a minority of scholars today that Jesus saw himself as the Servant of the Lord, destined to suffer, die, and be vindicated on behalf of sinful Israel. But it can hardly be doubted that Jesus did define his own destiny in scriptural terms.

For Paul, Jesus was not only the Messiah and the Servant of the Lord, but also a pre-existent figure who came down from heaven in order to redeem mankind. We will take one example of Paul's christocentric exegesis, which also incidentally illustrates how far he was dependent on traditional interpretation of scripture. In Romans 10.5–8 Paul writes as follows: 'Moses writes that the man who practises the righteousness that is based on the law shall live by it. But the righteousness based on faith says, Do not say in your heart, "Who will ascend into heaven?" (that is, to bring Christ down), or "Who will descend into the abyss?" (that is, to bring Christ up from the dead). But what does it say? The word is near you, on your lips and in your heart (that is, the word of faith which we preach).' Paul here quotes Deuteronomy 30.12–14, a passage intended to reassure Israel that the law was not difficult to perform. It was not in heaven so that someone should have to bring it down. It was not across the sea (Paul has altered the original text here) so that someone should have to cross the sea to fetch it back. It was there, close to Israel's heart. But Paul interprets the passage as referring to Christ's coming down from heaven and his being raised from the dead. He was able to do this because there was a tradition, now discovered in the Targum of Palestine, that these verses referred to Moses bringing the Torah down from Mount Sinai, and to Jonah visiting Sheol while in the belly of the great fish – both actions done on behalf of Israel's welfare. All that Paul does is to take these two incidents as prophetic types of Christ's incarnation and resurrection. Thus Paul's christocentric exegesis has enabled him to turn what was originally a passage commending law-observation into one which refers to the great saving events of Christ's career.

In Mark 4.12 we have a good example of how one synoptic writer uses scripture. He attributes to Jesus a quotation from Isaiah 6.9–10. It is a favourite quotation with New Testament writers as it is used also by Luke and John (Luke 19.42; Acts 28.26–27; John 12.40, and of course the parallels to this occurrence, Matt. 13.14–15 and Luke 8.10). It is probable that the quotation is part of Mark's editing or to his source rather than to Jesus himself. The statement of the incredulity which Isaiah's message encountered in his day is taken as a prophecy of the refusal of most Jews to believe in Jesus as the Messiah. Another excellent example of christological interpretation in the synoptics is Matthew 12.15–21, where the author of the First Gospel applies Isaiah 42.1–4 to Jesus' ministry, culminating in his cross and resurrection. The author actually makes use of an LXX mistranslation. See 12.20c 'till he brings justice to victory'. The Hebrew means 'till he has established justice in the earth'. The LXX by importing the idea of victory has made the citation more appropriate to the resurrection. This is one of Matthew's happier applications of Old Testament prophecy.

The Epistle to the Hebrews is so full of scripture quotations and allusions that one hardly knows which to choose by way of illustration. A good example occurs in Hebrews 2.5–13. Here the author begins by applying Psalm 8.5–7 to Jesus as representative man. He finds in the citation a reference to the incarnation ('Thou didst make him for a little while lower than the angels' – a LXX mistranslation has helped here), and he also finds an allusion to the resurrection-ascension: 'thou has crowned him with glory and honour.' There is also, the author believes, a reference to the *parousia*, 'putting everything in subjection under his feet'. This has not yet happened, he explains (Heb. 2.8). The author follows this up with a quotation from Psalm 22.22, which he understands as an utterance of the risen Christ present in the church's worship. Next comes a quotation of Isaiah 8.17–18, wherein, the author believes, Christ expresses his faith in the Father and acknowledges the members of the church as his spiritual children. Though we may well wonder how the author of Hebrews could persuade himself that Psalm 8 and Isaiah 8.17–18 really referred to all these events connected with the career of Christ, we can clearly see running through the passage the determinedly christocentric interpretation of scripture which is common to all the main writers of the New Testament.

For the Fourth Gospel we choose a quotation that is interesting because it is in all probability based on the Hebrew rather than on the Greek of the Old Testament. In John 1.14 the evangelist writes of the Word made flesh thus: 'And the Word became flesh and dwelt among us, full of grace and truth.' That phrase 'full of grace and truth' is a fairly accurate translation of a phrase in Exodus 34.6, where God grants to Moses a partial revelation of himself. He manifests himself as 'The Lord, a God merciful and gracious, slow to anger, and *abounding in steadfast love and faithfulness*'. The phrase in italics has been translated by John with the words in Greek 'full of grace and truth'. His rendering is quite unlike that of the LXX, but is in fact quite close to the Hebrew. The word which the RSV translators have rendered with 'steadfast love' in Exodus 34.6 is in Hebrew *hesed*; and the word translated 'faithfulness', in Hebrew *'emeth*, is often rendered 'truth' where it occurs elsewhere in the Old Testament. This is an immensely significant piece of scriptural interpretation by John. He is in effect claiming that he who revealed himself partially to Moses on the holy mountain of old was none other than he who appeared among men as Jesus Christ. This is one of the not infrequent passages in the Fourth Gospel where the Son is presented as a pre-existent being.

Finally, we should look at one example of the scriptural interpretation of St John the Divine, author of the Book of Revelation. His exegesis is just as christocentric as that of the others, but his technique is different. We choose Revelation 5.5–7. We must bear in mind that this writer never says 'thus was fulfilled the word of the prophet . . .'. He simply takes scriptural symbols and images and applies them to the entire career of Christ. Here for instance the 'scroll written within and on the back' of 5.1 comes from Ezekiel 2.9–10. It signifies God's future purpose for his people. Only Christ has the ability to carry out this purpose, because he has 'conquered' (Rev. 5.5), i.e. by his resurrection he has overcome death. He is described as 'the Lion of the tribe of Judah and the Root of David', both phrases taken from scripture, the first from Genesis 49.9 and the second from Isaiah 11.1. He is called 'a Lamb standing as though it had been slain' (verse 6) in order to emphasize his sacrificial death. The allusion is to Isaiah 53.7, where the obedient Servant of the Lord is compared to 'a lamb that is led to the slaughter'. His seven horns and seven eyes symbolize his power and his endowment with the Spirit (as the author indeed explains). The seven horns may come from Daniel 7.7–8, where the horns are the characteristics of powerful heathen empires. The Lamb is more powerful than they, but in a quite different mode. The seven eyes come from Zechariah 4.10, where they signify the all-seeing providence of God, an attribute now belonging to the victorious Lamb. Thus in a few verses John the Divine has claimed for Jesus Christ by virtue of his death and resurrection messiahship and divine status; and it is all done by the use of images taken directly from scripture.

IV

One's first reaction after having examined some typical specimens of the New Testament writers' interpretation of the Old Testament may well be one of dismay. How far is their technique from our modern notions of how the Bible ought to be understood! Surely we today cannot be expected to endorse their methods? But if not, what have we in common with them? We must ask the reader to reserve judgment until we come to the chapter on prophecy, where these matters are fairly dealt with. Suffice it to say that we do maintain the existence of something in common between them and us, enough for us to be able to share basically the same Christian faith.

That leaves us with the other point we have made in this section: there is no such thing as an uninterpreted Bible. We cannot appeal straight back to the Bible, ignoring the church's tradition. The Bible always has been an interpreted text. If we do not accept the church's interpretation we will only have to accept someone else's. You cannot come to the Bible with no presuppositions. When the Reformers insisted on *sola scriptura* (only the Bible as norm and not the church's tradition), they did not mean this to be taken too literally. If we examine what the great theologians of the Reformation meant by their appeal back to the Bible against the church's tradition, we find that they were appealing against the tradition of the contemporary Western church, not against the tradition of the church universal. As a matter of fact they were quite content with the tradition of the church of the first few centuries, and they certainly had no intention of repudiating the doctrinal foundation which had been laid by the church during the period up to at least AD 451, the year of the Council of Chalcedon, by which time the church's doctrine of both the incarnation and the Trinity had been largely decided.

We must therefore spend the rest of this chapter in determining what we mean by the church's interpretation of scripture. Our first point is simple enough: we are in a different position to that of the writers of the New Testament. They had to decide what was important for Christians in the Old Testament. We do not need to do this over again. No matter how bizarre their methods of interpretation appear to us today, they have made sufficiently clear what parts of the Old Testament Christians find relevant. We do not deny that we today know a great deal more about the circumstances in which the Old Testament was written than did the New Testament writers. But we do not need to challenge their judgment about the significance of the Old Testament for Christians.

We are, however, left with a Bible that consists of both Old Testament and New Testament. What do we mean when we claim that Christians can accept the church's interpretation of that Bible? We mean in essence that the way in which the church through the ages has interpreted the Bible is right. This is not a claim that the church can interpret every verse and solve every problem for us. The church as a whole has never attempted to do this, and if one were to consult all the competent authorities through the ages on any one question of biblical interpretation, one would receive a completely diverse answer. What we may accept is the church's understanding of the main drift of the Bible, what some of the Fathers called its 'scope', what Luther called its 'Trieb', its drive or main intention. There is no great mystery about this. The drive or drift of the Bible is summed up in the church's creeds, very sketchily in the Apostles' Creed, much more fully in the Nicene-Constantinopolitan Creed which the majority of the members of the church still recite today when they attend the celebration of the eucharist.

This of course leaves an immense range of biblical interpretation still to be undertaken, and this always will be so. The daily task of explaining and exploring scripture in detail for the benefit of believers is one which always has to be undertaken by those in the church who are competent to do so. At this precise point in the church's history we are very happy that scholars of all Christian traditions and denominations are able to work at this task together. From the time of the Reformation in the middle of the sixteenth century until the middle of the present century, this was not the case at all. There was a sharp division between Catholic and Protestant scholars on this very question of biblical interpretation. Although there are still areas in which Catholic and reformed find themselves in disagreement, they are few and by no means incapable of an eirenic solution. It may be quite truthfully said that what divides Roman Catholics from the rest of Western Christendom is not the question of how the Bible should be interpreted. For this (*sub Deo*) we have the ecumenical movement to thank.

There is, however, still a residual element in the Roman Catholic Church that would like to keep the interpretation of scripture much more fully under the control of the rulers of the church than it is at present. If you discuss the interpretation of scripture with well informed members of the Roman Catholic Church, one of them will probably refer sooner or later to what is called the church's *magisterium*, the teaching office of the church. You will be told that in the last resort only the hierarchy, headed by the Pope, has the right to decide matters concerning faith and morals in the church. This is not perhaps precisely a claim that only they know how the Bible should be interpreted. But, since both faith and morals are supposed to be based on scripture, it amounts to this. This distinction between the teaching church (i.e. the hierarchy) and the learning church (i.e. the laity) is quite a recent one. It was not heard of before the beginning of the nineteenth century. The distinction was no doubt originally made in the face of the intellectual impact of the Enlightenment on the church, followed by that child of Enlightenment, biblical criticism. When scholars and theologians, influenced by these movements, whether Catholic or Protestant, began to draw some of the conclusions in the area of biblical interpretation and doctrine which both the presuppositions of the Enlightenment and the results of biblical criticism seemed to require, the hierarchy in alarm began to insist on this doctrine of the *magisterium*. Only the official teachers of the church, it was claimed, knew how the Bible ought to be interpreted. No Catholic must disagree with their conclusions.

As long as the debate was maintained at a general level, not much damage was done. But by the end of the nineteenth century biblical criticism had been making quite striking progress among reformed Christians and was beginning to be accepted in some degree by Roman Catholic scholars. This resulted in the establishment by Pope Leo XIII in 1902 of a Biblical Commission. This was a body composed of high-ranking members of the hierarchy, all of whom had impressive-sounding degrees in biblical studies and theology from Roman Catholic universities, but almost none of whom knew very much about the new criticism. The purpose of the Commission was to give authoritative rulings on all matters concerning the Bible that were troubling Catholics. This was a new departure. Never before had any section of the church undertaken to provide authoritative guidance on the details of biblical interpretation. At the time of its establishment it was hailed by many Roman Catholics as an admirable development: now Roman Catholics would be able to solve all those doubts and difficulties which were causing so much trouble to Protestants, who were not blessed by the possession of an authoritarian system of government.

The Biblical Commission, however, proved to be a disastrous failure. This is not because the members of the Commission hesitated to give answers to the disputed questions. On the contrary, they gave rulings and conclusion on many of the burning issues of the day with the most superb confidence. Unfortunately, however, the answers almost invariably proved to be wrong. The best Roman Catholic scholars of the time (none of whom figured on the Commission) knew they were wrong, and it is now universally and openly admitted by all scholars in the Roman Catholic Church that they were wrong. The Bible Commission has been wound up, and replaced by a Pontifical Biblical Institute staffed by very well qualified scholars, who appear to be under no restraint from the Vatican. The Institute is making a most valuable contribution to our understanding of the Bible, but it wisely refrains from making the authoritarian claims made on behalf of its predecessor.

The moral is surely that the church as such can only give very general guidance about the meaning of the Bible. It is not fitted *as an institution* to give daily and detailed guidance. For this Christians must have recourse, as they always have in the past, to those best fitted to help them, the scholars and theologians who have mastered the techniques of modern study of the Bible, whether they are clergy or laity. The faithful, however, have no reason to complain that they are left in the dark about how to interpret the Bible. As long as we hold to the main drift of the Bible as understood by the church down the ages, and that means in effect the doctrines of the incarnation, the atonement, and the Trinity, we will not go far wrong.

Chapter Four

The Interpretation of the Bible in the Early Church

The ancient world liked oracles. In classical Greece of the fifth and fourth centuries BC the Delphic oracle had very great influence in both political and personal affairs. Other oracles, such as that of Zeus in Dodona and of Zeus Ammon in Egypt, were esteemed nearly as highly. Aristophanes in his comedy *The Birds* introduces an itinerant oracle-monger among those who visit the new state in the sky. Though by the time Christianity appeared on the scene in the early Roman Empire the great oracles had lost much of their reputation, and some like Dodona had ceased to function, oracles of various sorts were still very popular. Lucian, the pagan satirist of the second century AD, tells the story of an astute character named Alexander who set up an oracle in a little town in Asia Minor called Abounoteichos and did very well out of it. He made a lot of money and was able to marry off his daughter well. He held a great annual festival at which he officially warned off Christians among others. Jewish propaganda in the second and third centuries had circulated a large number of spurious *Sibylline Oracles*, pronouncements in hexameter lines alleged to have been uttered at some time or another by a succession of inspired prophetesses at oracles. Christians were impressed by this type of propaganda, and duly imitated it, producing a series of passages of the same type supposed to have been uttered by sibyls in favour of Christianity. Porphyry, the New-Platonic philosopher of the third century who was a dedicated and highly intelligent opponent of Christianity, attempted to compose a kind of pagan *summa theologiae* by weaving together the various utterances attributed to pagan oracles in the ancient world. Roman Emperors were very sensitive about the possibility that malevolent-minded people might ascertain by means of preternatural investigation how long they were destined to reign. Plutarch, a learned pagan intellectual of the second century A D, devoted a whole treatise to a serious study of how the Pythian prophetess at Delphi, who was still functioning though in a rather reduced way in his day, could be inspired. His work is reminiscent of a Victorian ecclesiastic of liberal views trying to explain how the Bible can be inspired, in spite of historical criticism. Origen the Christian theologian of the third century, certainly believed that the prophetess at Delphi is inspired to foretell the future, but gives as disreputable an account of how it happens as he can think of. Sibyls and oracles of all sorts, in his view and in the view of all the Christians of his time, are inspired by filthy daemons, and good Christians should have nothing to do with them.

It is not surprising, therefore, that the people of the early church should have treated the scriptures, and particularly the scriptures of the Old Testament, as essentially oracular documents. The delusion survives still in our own day. On several occasions the writers of the New Testament describe parts of the Old Testament as 'oracles' (*logia*), e.g. Acts 7.38, Rom. 3.2 and Heb. 5.12. To accord this treatment to the Bible had the double advantage of commending to the Gentile world, brought up in Graeco-Roman culture, a series of sacred writings which that culture would otherwise have found somewhat incomprehensible and even uncongenial, and also of leaving comfortably unexplained the more obscure passages in the Old Testament. Nobody expects oracles to be luminously clear.

In short, the ancient church treated the Bible as if it were a series of oracles, sacred, obscure, full of hidden, ambiguous, wonderful, secret knowledge, to be decoded by the Christian, and especially by the Christian theologian. Origen was one of the most voluminous commentators on scripture of the ancient church, and it is amazing to observe his attitude to scripture, not least in one of his most recently discovered works, the *Peri Pascha* (*On the Passover*). He gazes into the text like a scientist gazing into the depths of some Caribbean lagoon which conceals all sorts of zoological wonders. For Origen, all wisdom is in the scriptures, all knowledge, theological, scientific, philosophic and spiritual. Layer after layer of concealed wisdom is to be deciphered there. The same attitude, though perhaps not so intensely held nor ingenuously displayed, can be found in virtually all the theologians of the ancient church.

One of the results of this attitude is a deplorable atomization of the Bible. Oracles are not usually delivered as continuous passages of connected argument, but as mysterious separate unconnected utterances. The ancient writers consequently think themselves entitled to wrench any text out of its context and apply it directly to whatever purpose they deem fit, regardless of the surrounding material. The great text which sounds continually through the Arian controversy of the fourth century is Proverbs 8.22, which was of course given a christological meaning. A verse from the Old Testament was chosen as the supremely significant statement about the divine status of Jesus Christ! The great text regarded as crucial for the divinity of the Holy Spirit in the same century was Amos 4.13 (wrongly translated)! Any passage in any part of the Old or New Testaments was liable to be pulled right out of its context and applied incontinently to the advanced theological developments of the fourth century. One could perhaps modify this judgment by saying that the Fathers interpret the Bible as a whole, but this would be true only in the sense that they use the Bible as a sort of glossary. They will range over the whole scriptures hunting one word or one idea, making no allowance for author or context. For instance, Lucifer of Calaris in the sixties of the fourth century ransacks the Bible to find examples of wicked kings with whom he can compare the Emperor Constantius II, but he does so indiscriminately and uncritically. And Origen will take some theme like 'wine' or 'bull' and pluck examples of its use from all over the Bible, wringing by means of allegory every last possible and impossible meaning from it that will suit his particular very sophisticated theological ideas. But it still holds true that the Fathers' treatment of the Bible is essentially atomic. It rests upon the assumption, of course, that there is a pretty similar level of inspiration and revelation to be found in every part of the text.

There are a few minor exceptions to this assumption of a single level of revelation. Gregory of Nazianzus, for instance, realized that the doctrine of the Son in the Old Testament was, to say the least, undeveloped, and that the doctrine of the Holy Spirit in the New Testament was also undeveloped, and to this last proposition Basil of Caesarea would have assented. Both these writers realized that the Bible needs amplifying and developing in the light of the experience of the church. Similarly, many writers from the fourth century onwards are ready to argue from the practice of baptism and from the eucharist, which is a kind of admission that the Bible is not an omnicompetent encyclopedia. But these are relatively small exceptions to what can safely be regarded as a general rule.

The ancient interpreters of the Bible, however, are not literalists in the sense that modern fundamentalists are. The Neo-Arian Eunomius insisted in one of his works that the words recorded of God in the early chapters of Genesis were actually and audibly spoken by God to Adam and the serpent, and Gregory of Nyssa, replying to his arguments, jeered at Eunomius for his crudeness in this. Augustine was ready to believe that the 'days' of creation were really long ages, and others before him had suggested this. For the most part the early theologians are not troubled by inconsistencies or contradictions to be found in the Bible. Porphyry in his anti-Christian work had pointed out several, especially in the gospels, and Eusebius of Caesarea and Augustine labour to explain them away. The subject of chronology especially occupied the minds of the more learned of the Fathers, such as Julius Africanus and Eusebius of Caesarea. They try to collate the chronology of the biblical narratives with what they knew of the chronology of ancient history before them, and in the process gave the impetus to the study of world history. But a serious attempt to harmonize all the contradictions and inconsistencies in the Bible was never made. The main reason for this was that the ancient Christian writers thought that they had at hand a convenient tool for reconciling all difficulties in the application of allegorization to the sacred text. Origen indeed positively drew attention to the inconsistencies in the gospels in order to underline the advantage of allegorizing them away. But in this he was untypical.

As we try to estimate the biblical interpretation of the writers of the early church, we must realize the conditions and the limitations under which they worked. Almost all of them read the Old Testament in translation, as we do. The Greek-speakers read the Septuagint for the most part, a translation of varying fidelity according to the book, or even the part of the book, translated, some of it good, some of it almost unintelligible. The Latin-speakers read a bad translation of this Greek translation. It was not till about AD 400 that a translation by Jerome direct from the Hebrew was available, and even then this new version, which ultimately became the Latin Vulgate, only made its way slowly into the lectionaries and the minds of conservative Christians. The necessity of reading the Old Testament in translation (and for the Latin-speakers, the New Testament too) cast a kind of mist round the text, so that the readers were receiving it at one remove from reality, so to speak. At Isaiah 51.20 the prophet says that the sons of Israel, exhausted and fainting, 'lie at the top of every street like an antelope in a net'. The LXX translator found the Hebrew too much for him here, and made a wild guess at the meaning. His translation means 'like a half-cooked piece of beetroot' (*hōs seutlion hēmiephthon*). At Amos 4.13 Amos apostrophizes God as 'he who forms the mountains and creates the wind and declares to man what is his thought'. This was mistranslated by the LXX translator to mean in its last clause 'and declares to man his Christ'. The Christian theologians found the temptation to see a christological reference here irresistible, especially as the Greek word for 'wind' was the same as the word for Spirit – *pneuma*. A little mistranslation, a little manipulating and we find Amos making an impeccably Trinitarian statement! Another well-known example of the mischief done by mistranslation is the rendering in the gospels of the frequent exhortation to repent: the Latin often rendered it 'do penance' (*facite paenitentiam*), thereby importing into it important undertones which were not originally there. A curious phenomenon of early Christian interpretation was the tendency for additions which were not originally there to creep into the sacred text. The *Comma Johanneum* is probably the best-known, whereby an interpolator working in the third or fourth century slipped into the text of the fifth chapter of the First Epistle of John some plainly Trinitarian words which the original author had certainly not written (see I John 5.7–8). This egregious piece of forgery was nourished devoutly in the Western Church and still appeared in the *Book of Common Prayer* and the King James Version. A more innocent error is the statement of Justin Martyr in the middle of the second century that one of the Psalms had declared that 'the Lord shall reign from a tree', which Justin took to be a prophecy by David of the crucifixion of Jesus Christ. No psalm in the Psalter makes any such statement; it is likely that the word *Selah* (whose meaning has long been forgotten) appearing at the end of a psalm which declared that 'the Lord shall reign' was corrupted by a translator into the Greek word for a tree (*xylon*) and that pious ignorance did the rest. A few writers, such as Origen, Eusebius of Caesarea and Eusebius of Emesa, knew that the original of the Old Testament had been written in Hebrew, but most behaved as if the Greek was the original, and most believed some version of the legend about its being made miraculously by seventy different translators who arrived at exactly the same result.

Most ancient commentators on the Bible had been taught rhetoric, which included some appreciation of prose style, though we can find exceptions to this rule, such as Victorinus of Pettau and Lucifer of Calaris. They consequently tended to find the style of the writers of the Old and New Testaments strange and inelegant, and sometimes felt obliged to apologize for it. It was the characteristic which repelled pagans from Christianity perhaps more than any other. It repelled Augustine for long.

The attitude of the ancient commentators to variant readings in the manuscripts of the Bible is curious. Sometimes they used them to evade difficulties. Origen finds that the evangelist at Luke 23.45 apparently says that at the crucifixion of Christ 'the sun was eclipsed' (*hēliou ekleipontos*). He knows that an eclipse of the sun at Passover-time is impossible, so he prefers the alternative reading, which is not nearly as well attested as the other, 'the sun was darkened', i.e. was obscured by clouds. But when Eusebius of Caesarea is interpreting the Psalms, and using not merely more than one manuscript, but several different translations of the Hebrew as well, he chooses whichever translation or reading makes better sense, that is, sense for a Christian interpreter, not simply the LXX. On the whole, however, when faced with alternative readings, ancient commentators tended to interpret both without making any choice between them.

We must remember that almost nobody in the ancient world had the Bible as a single book. Either as a collection of separate scrolls or as a codex it would have been far too bulky to transport as a whole Bible. When Jesus is represented as 'beginning with Moses and all the prophets and interpreting to them in all the scriptures the things concerning himself', we must not imagine him as taking a Bible out from beneath his robes and opening it. What Augustine had at hand in the famous episode of his conversion in the garden in Milan was a single copy of St Paul's Epistle to the Romans, not even a New Testament. This necessity of taking the Bible book by book must have contributed to form their atomizing approach to the scriptures. The ancient commentators and theologians certainly knew their Bible very well, quite as well as did the men and women of the Reformation. And this knowledge included the Apocrypha, between which and the rest of scriptures they (very reasonably, in our view) made virtually no distinction at all. They can range through the whole Bible when necessary with ease, knowing it, we must conclude, largely by memory. In some cases they certainly had lists of proof-texts to assist them. In at least one of his books Cyprian is certainly using such a work inherited from his predecessors. They had at their disposal etymological lists of scriptural names (largely fallacious) whose use goes back to Judaism. They may have used glossaries of biblical words detailing their use throughout the Bible, but only further research can determine this. They can also use verses or passages which are not exactly additions to the text but which are so widely different from all versions known to us that they are almost so, like the text allegedly from Isaiah used both in I Clement (42.5) and in Irenaeus as a proof-text for supporting the existing form of the ministry, 'I shall set up their bishops in righteousness and their deacons in faith' (see Isa. 60.17), or the very widely used conflation of two Johannine texts, 'I and the Father who sent me are One' (see John 5.37 and 10.30).

This oracular approach to the Bible blinded the ancient theologians to certain important points. One result of this attitude was their extraordinary failure to appreciate the literary quality of the Bible. They were incapable for instance of realizing that the Book of Job is a great dramatic poem, though several commentaries on his book survive from the Patristic period. They could not appreciate the poetry of the Book of Isaiah, nor of the Psalms. Faced, for instance, with the words in Psalm 22.6: 'But I am a worm and no man', Origen, unable to understand the vivid Hebrew metaphor, makes the amazingly dense comment that because worms beget their kind without sexual intercourse this must be a reference to the virginal conception of Christ. Eusebius of Caesarea was the best Christian scholar of his day, but as he deals with the Psalms he again and again fails to perceive and make allowance for poetic diction and imagery. This is all the more surprising because, as we have seen, most of the ancient writers had had a rhetorical training. Augustine, the most successful rhetor of them all, can elaborately allegorize the parable of the Good Samaritan. In this case their reverence for the biblical text misled them. They could not admit seriously that these books were the product of human minds. The result was a great deal of ponderous and even learned nonsense. Their other presuppositions also vitiated their hermeneutics: the theory which we have already examined that the Psalms are christological discourse by David including, *inter alia*, something like taped recordings of conversations between the Father and the Son, and their insistence that the prophets were uttering Christian doctrine hundreds of years before the advent of Christ. Sometimes they manage to extract a meaning which is precisely the opposite of the meaning intended in the text, as when they twist Job's emphatic denial of the possibility of man surviving death into a statement of his belief in such a survival, or interpret the question of Jesus at Mark 10.18, 'Why do you call me good? No one is good but God alone' as a claim on the part of Jesus to be God. Athanasius, among others, can say that when Christ professes ignorance he is only pretending to be ignorant, because he must have been omniscient. Hilary, plunging into Docetism, can allege that Jesus did not feel the pain of his suffering. The Fathers were to some extent necessarily uncritical in their treatment of the Bible, because they did not possess the criticial tools available to modern scholars, but their oracular approach made them extravagantly uncritical. Porphyry the pagan was capable of making percipient remarks of a critical nature about the gospels of which many Christian theologians would have been incapable. Plutarch in the second century can sometimes treat the ancient narratives which he uses to compose his *Lives* in a manner which might have given the Christians a good example in dealing with the ancient stories in the Old Testament had they chosen to follow his example. Porphyry also perceived the actual date and purpose of the Book of Daniel sixteen hundred years before modern scholarship entirely endorsed his judgment.

Much of the Fathers' defects in interpreting the Bible resulted from the seductive possibility of using allegory to overcome difficulties. Had this all too useful tool not been available to them, they might have exercised their intellects to better advantage upon the text and been compelled to face the problems presented in it more realistically. There is a fashion in some quarters today to defend the Fathers' use of allegory and even to claim that it is an essential part of Christian hermeneutics. We cannot endorse this view. The use of allegory in interpreting scripture must be regarded, on a long view, as a disaster and as contributing largely to the creation of many unnecessary illusions. It preserved the ancients, indeed, from fundamentalism, but it prevented them from approaching the text with proper rigour, with a determination to examine the actual, original meaning carefully and thoroughly. The use of allegory was not merely unhistorical, it was anti-historical. It militated against any attempt to take texts in their historical context and relate them to their background. Origen, for instance, in dealing with the Pentateuchal legislation, comes upon a mention of a frying-pan. How can we conceive, he asks, of Almighty God in conversing with Moses on Mount Sinai descending to such a ridiculously unimportant object as a frying-pan? It must conceal some deeper, more profound meaning, and he proceeds to allegorize it. And when he comes in his *Commentary on Jeremiah* to the historical notes which give the dates, calculating by the regnal years of the kings of Judah, of the particular utterances or acts of the prophet, he cannot see what possible relevance they can have to the Christian dispensation; they must be allegorized. Allegory was a mist through which they looked at scripture, and they could not see it clearly. They inherited this tradition of allegorizing from Judaism before them, of course, and they found allegory used (but not to any good purpose) in the New Testament. But, assisted by the example given by Philo, they allowed the practice to run riot, they were intoxicated by it. And, like all excessive indulgence in a stimulating drug, it betrayed them.

After surveying all these defects and distortions in the ancient tradition of interpreting the Bible, we may well wonder how they ever succeeded in understanding scripture, wandering as they were too often in the miasma of allegory, pursuing the will-o-the-wisp of christological interpretation. They had, however, certain advantages on their side. They knew, at least the Easterners knew Greek, the language of the New Testament, much better than we ever could because it was their native language, but the language had changed to some extent since the time when the New Testament was written. They were, virtually to a man, pastors as well as theologians. The chasm which now divides the scholar in the lecture hall from the parson in the pulpit and the laity in the pew did not exist for them. In spite of their hermeneutical vagaries, they were open to certain forces which tended to give an outline and a structure to their doctrine and keep it within reasonable bounds, the liturgy, the Rule of Faith, the Creed, all of them derived from or heavily influenced by the Bible. Sometimes we can see the Bible as it were forcing its meaning on them in spite of their tendency to misunderstand it. Athanasius understood the basic intention of the Gospel according to St John, even though his interpretation of it is often strained, and this enabled him to take the lead in the doctrinal development of the fourth century and to guide the church through a theological revolution which threw off some dangerous ideas influenced by contemporary Greek philosophy and to achieve the doctrine of God as the Holy Trinity. Augustine had been taught the far-fetched theory that the Psalter represented advanced Christian doctrine divined by David centuries and centuries before Christ. But the very nature of the Psalms compelled him to recognize them as utterances of souls directly facing God in an existential encounter, remote from christological fantasies, and as such they entered deeply into his thought and spirituality. No serious theologian in the ancient church could ignore the fact that the historical character of the witness to revelation found in the Bible meant that God was radically concerned with history, and above all in the incarnation. This conviction was one which did not agree with the Greek philosophy in which most of the old writers had been brought up, but they never attempted to evade it. The fact that in the development of the doctrine of the Trinity the fourth-century theologians finally decided that it is necessary to believe in the Godhead of the Holy Spirit is a tribute to their fidelity to scripture.

Philosophy did not demand this doctrine, but a careful understanding of the scripture did.

Most impressive perhaps is the fact that the ancient Fathers grasped firmly and never betrayed what we might call the main burden or drift or message of the Bible, however fantastic may have been their misunderstanding of its details. They recognized the necessity of comprehending this 'burden' and used various words for it: Tertullian called it the *ratio*, Irenaeus the *hypothesis* and Athanasius the *skopos*. Once they had distanced themselves a little from the entrancing details, the deceptive individual trees, they saw the shape of the wood clearly enough. When they withdrew a little from the intoxicating business of allegorizing the details, they then perceived the true import of the Bible, undistracted by philosophy, undrugged by allegory. There is perhaps a moral for us today in this achievement.

Chapter Five

Historical Criticism of the Bible

I

The basic assumptions both of the ancient exegetes and of the men of the Reformation were destroyed by the growth of historical criticism. This is a method of handling historical documents which had its roots both in the Renaissance and the Reformation, but which was fed from several other sources, such as the Enlightenment and the Romantic Movement. Its basic idea was the simple one that historical documents are the product of their own time and not of ours. It entailed an achievement of historical perspective which was very largely lacking in the ancient world and in the Middle Ages. It is excellently illustrated by the contrast between mediaeval representations of biblical scenes in painting and sculpture and glass, where all the characters wear clothes such as the contemporaries of the artist or craftsman wore, and similar representations of the nineteenth and twentieth centuries, when efforts, sometimes dismally unsuccessful, are made to clothe the characters in the garments of their own day. From this simple axiom sprang one of the most prolific and active disciplines of our day, that of the study of history, and with it there came into existence a galaxy of allied disciplines such as archaeology, textual criticism, numismatology and economic, social and aesthetic history. The study of history, which up to the eighteenth century had been regarded as a minor aid to the practice of oratory, to which it could furnish useful examples, developed in revolutionary fashion and brought with it an ineluctable revolution in the study of the Bible.

This revolution was only appreciated slowly in the English-speaking world. As so often it was first nourished for the most part in Germany, and only reached Britain and America later. A conventional date for its arrival in the limelight is usually taken to be the publication of the composite volume *Essays and Reviews* in 1860. This was a volume of essays written by well-known Church of England clergy and laity advocating a moderate use of biblical criticism. It caused a huge upset among leading churchmen. Its authors were denounced as traitors to the Christian faith. Ever since then, historical criticism of the Bible has been a controversial but essential part of the studies of any competent theological student.

The use of allegory was in fact not merely unhistorical but anti-historical. With historical criticism the pendulum swings the other way. The first essential to the understanding of any passage in the Bible must be to discover, as far as possible, when it was written. The result of this technique was, naturally, the discovery that the documents of the Bible were no less, but also no more, accurate and historically reliable than similar documents of the age and of the culture in which they were written. This meant, for instance, that as every part of the Bible was written many centuries before the advent of modern science it could give us no authoritative information about those facts with which science is capable of dealing. The Book of Genesis was found to contain virtually no history at all, and to give us no reliable information whatever about the age of the universe, the origin of mankind and the beginning of civilization. One of the most startling results of the application of historical criticism was the revision which it necessitated in our ideas as to who the writers of the Bible were. In the traditional view the Bible had been written by a comparatively small number of people, perhaps twenty or thirty: Moses, David, Solomon, Ezra, Isaiah, Jeremiah, Ezekiel, Daniel, the twelve Minor Prophets, the Four Evangelists, Paul, Peter, Jude and a very few more. Historical criticism demolished this view: Moses had not written the Pentateuch nor David the Psalms nor Solomon the Books of Proverbs and Ecclesiastes, nor Matthew and John the Apostles the Gospels attributed to them, nor Paul the Epistle to the Hebrews, nor the Pastoral Epistles. The Book of Daniel was not written by a mystic predictor in the seventh century BC, but by a commentator on contemporary history in the second. The Bible was divided up among a host of anonymous sources. Apparent history was in many cases discovered to be fable or saga or myth. Samson disappeared into a sun-myth. The historical existence of Abraham, of Joseph, of Esther became highly precarious. Evidence for miracles recorded in the Old Testament was completely discredited. Joshua had not stopped the sun nor Balaam conversed with his ass, nor Jonah had that remarkable experience with the whale.* It became completely impossible to regard the Bible as an infallible or inerrant book in any meaningful sense.

The advent of historical criticism meant that the Bible, along with all other historical movements of any sort, had to be treated in an analytical, critical manner before it could be used positively and constructively. Before this, history had been used analogously, to provide situations similar to those which we encounter in contemporary experience, from which we can learn something to enable us to cope with the situations of our own day. Newman still treats history in this way in his *Essay on The Development of Christian Doctrine.* But now critical analysis was the first rule of historical study. And critical analysis of the Bible produced startling and disturbing results. It meant, for instance, that David had not slain Goliath, but an obscure character called Elhanan the son of Jaareoregim (II Sam. 21.19) had done so. It meant that Job, far from being an outstanding example of patience, as the author of the epistle of James (5.11) along with a full chorus of Patristic and mediaeval authorities claimed, stood out as a daring and disconcerting challenger of the justice of God, an Old Testament Prometheus. Its results on the New Testament were more drastic still. An analysis of the evidence for the virgin birth of Jesus left the probability of that event weak. A critical comparison of the Fourth Gospel with the synoptic gospels, which has now been under way for nearly two centuries, has not resulted in the establishment of St John's Gospel as a wholly reliable historical account of the words and acts of Jesus when matched with the first three. On the contrary, though scholarship has not dismissed the Fourth Gospel as a late Hellenistic document wholly devoted to overlaying the original story with the categories of Greek thought, as was at one time suggested, it looks very much as if this gospel is rather an interpretation of the significance of Jesus Christ, like the epistles of Paul, than a largely historical account. And this has far-ranging results for our understanding of the christology of the New Testament. Perhaps more inward still, we cannot any longer accept uncritically as clearly right the manner in which the writers of the New Testament identify prophecies of Christ in the Old. We must in a strict survey reject the majority of them as fanciful rather than convincing, and not least that most used one of all, Isaiah 7.14ff., where the so-called 'virgin' is not a

*The credibility of Genesis and the edibility of Jonah were alike questioned in an epigram uttered by Ronald Knox, a witty Cambridge don who could not stand the strain of criticism and took refuge in the Roman Catholic Church, which at that time (the 1920s) seemed to be unaffected by these destructive ideas concerning the Bible.

virgin at all but a young married woman. The Jewish scholars, who all through the centuries maintained this point against the Christians, were right and the Christians wrong. The most disturbing point of all is that New Testament scholarship has been for fifty years unable to supply us with any reliable criterion for determining which of the words attributed to Jesus in the gospels are authentic and which not. All that it can say with confidence is that they cannot all be authentic.

In this situation there are three alternatives open to us. We can resolutely shut our eyes to historical scholarship and refuse to have anything to do with it on the grounds that it comes from the devil. Another form of the same policy is to approach the Bible with all the apparent instruments of scholarship but always by some curious coincidence come to the most conservative conclusions. This entails so many ingenious but unconvincing explanations of each inconsistency or contradiction or error as it presents itself that this method can reasonably be described as dying the death of a thousand qualifications. This alternative should be, for all educated people who pay attention to their consciences, an impossible one. We cannot put back the clock of history and behave as if historical scholarship does not exist. We cannot cocoon ourselves in a world of fantasy where God walks in the garden in the cool of the evening, where Balaam converses with his donkey, where David and the prophets foretell to their own generation events and doctrines which have no relevance to anybody for the next thousand or six hundred years, where Jesus of Nazareth walks the lanes of Galilee and the streets of Jerusalem informing his hearers that he is God. Those who accept the discipline of historical criticism do so because their consciences tell them that they must accept truth. And to use this instrument having determined beforehand that it will deliver only the conservative and traditional conclusions is to palter with the truth and to corrupt the traditions of scholarship.

The second alternative is to conclude that the status and authority of the Bible are indeed completely exploded, that with the disappearance of the traditional doctrine of its inspiration (and certainly that doctrine has disappeared) no further use of the Bible remains for Christians. Many high-minded scholars in the last century took this path, wistfully acknowledging that now the authority of the Bible was in ruins. And many ordinary Christians have protested anxiously that if even one error or inconsistency is found in this sacred book, then the authority of the whole collapses. It is certainly true that when an oracle is found to be false it loses its authority. Is this what has happened to the 'lively oracles of God'?

We shall deal first with the last objection, that if one point in the sacred book is found false or unreliable, then the whole is discredited. This is one of the commonest, and also one of the silliest, difficulties which face people when they encounter historical criticism of the Bible. No reputable historian of the ancient (or indeed of the modern) world would think of abandoning any belief in a document simply because he found an error in it. If a historian is handling, for instance, Thucydides' *History of the Peloponnesian War*, or Plutarch's *Lives* or Plato's *Dialogues*, he would not on finding one error reject the whole as hopelessly unreliable. He would take each statement on its merits and determine the value of the whole by the document's reliability as a whole, not simply by one point alone. It is only if we make the unfounded and unnecessary assumption that the Bible is above error, a book exempted from error, that we can be thrown into a state of alarm and despondency by a single mistake, or indeed by several mistakes.

As we conclude our first examination of the nature of the Bible we must stress the fact that historical criticism of the Bible has meant an actual revolution in its interpretation. No revolution ever completely starts all over again, leaving no continuity with what went before; neither the French nor the Russian revolution achieved that, and of course the revolution caused by the advent of historical criticism did not destroy all common ground between exegesis before and exegesis after the revolution. We hope that the arguments put forward in this book make this sufficiently clear. But still historical criticism has effected a revolution in the interpretation of the Bible, a slow, creeping revolution, but a thorough one nevertheless. Nothing will ever be quite the same after it. We look at the biblical authors and at what they wrote in a new and different light from that in which our forefathers saw them.

This is a hard saying, and one from which clergy and church authorities of all sorts are liable to recoil in dismay. Intellectual courage is not, in our experience, an outstanding quality of clergy in the twentieth century, and in consequence the ordinary layman and laywoman in the pew and the intelligent reader outside the pew have been very ill served by those who are supposed to teach them the truths of religion. The impression has been widely spread that historical criticism really does not matter, that it can be ignored or left to the experts or the intellectuals and that as far as the Bible is concerned nothing important has changed. It is easy to allow that the Book of Jonah is fiction not history, rather less easy to assume the same about Adam and Eve, and not very painful to throw a veil of uncertainty over the early history of the people of Israel. But to suggest that David did not kill Goliath, but Elhanan did, that Isaiah did not write chapters 40–55 of the book attributed to him, and that Balaam did not converse with his donkey causes alarm and despondency and is not alluded to in sermon or Sunday School. Far less is criticism of the New Testament permitted to intrude into the ordinary teaching of the church. As far as this goes, in most parishes we might as well be living in 1789, not 1989. The idea that St John's Gospel is not straightforward reliable reporting, or that the New Testament is a record of a gradual, piecemeal, growing understanding of the significance of Jesus Christ, or that all the words attributed to Jesus in the gospels are not authentic and original, is kept rigorously concealed, either because the clergy have forgotten what they presumably learned during their theological education, or because they have not the courage nor the competence to face what they learned. They bury all such distressing ideas in the excuse that they do not want to disturb the faith of their people.

This book is written partly as a protest against this almost universal conspiracy to conceal the truth. We believe that God does not want us to conceal truth, that in the long run to hide the truth or to evade it under any plea is more destructive for the life of a Christian community than to allow truth to appear in the light of day. If anybody wants to see an object lesson in the results of such concealment, he should look at the present state of Christianity in Northern Ireland, where in the interests of sectarian strife almost all intellectual consideration of the Christian faith is being ignored or suppressed. Truth is often painful. David found the truth about his treatment of Uriah the Hittite as presented by Nathan painful. The seventeenth-century church found the truth about the celestial bodies as discovered by Galileo so painful that the authorities did their best to suppress it, so as not to disturb the faith of ordinary devout Christians. But timid conservatism is no proper companion for authentic Christian faith; yet timid conservatism is what largely prevails in the handling of the Bible among church-goers today. God may wish us to endure difficulty and disorientation in order that we may achieve a fuller understanding of his will. Truth may indeed be painful, but it can also be liberating!

II

Historical criticism of the Bible has challenged two widely held beliefs about it; that it is inerrant and that it is inspired. We must therefore now examine these two topics, the inerrancy and the inspiration of the Bible. In dealing with this we shall take as a representative view a book called *Theopneustia: The Divine Inspiration of the Bible* written originally in French by one L. Gaussens and translated into English and published in Edinburgh in 1841. It must have been considered a standard work because it was reprinted without alteration in Grand Rapids, Michigan, in 1971. How anyone could have thought that it constituted a useful contribution to the debate of inspiration one hundred and thirty years after the first appearance of its English version is difficult to imagine, for it is written in a tone of pious rhetoric which is far from suited to the atmosphere of discussion today, and the author is, of course, wholly unaware of modern developments in historical criticism of the Bible. But if some people in Grand Rapids thought it worth reprinting in 1971 we are entitled to regard it as a representative fundamentalist statement on the subject of inspiration. For other theories of inspiration we shall mainly use that admirable book *Catholic Theories of Inspiration since 1810*, written by J. T. Burtchaell and published in Cambridge, England, in 1969.

We must first, however, give the *coup de grace* to a widely-used argument in favour of the inspiration of the Bible which rests upon an easily detectable logical fallacy. This is the argument that the Bible is inspired because it says so (II Tim. 3.16–17; I Peter 1.10–12; II Peter 1.20–22; John 10.35; etc.). The strongest reason for rejecting this argument is that it contains a *petitio principii*, i.e. it assumes as part of the proof that which has to be proven. 'The Bible is inspired because the inspired Bible says so' is a way of putting the same proposition which brings out more clearly the fallacy contained in it. If we were to maintain that the *Communist Manifesto* of Marx and Engels was the last word in economic orthodoxy and beyond criticism, and on being challenged to support this extreme view we declared that the *Manifesto* itself said so, we would convince nobody. So this argument for the inspiration of the Bible must be decisively rejected.

Next we must insist that any argument in favour of biblical inspiration must show that the Bible is *uniquely* inspired, that its inspiration is not just like the kind of inspiration which we might attribute to a play by Euripides, a tragedy by Shakespeare or a great religious work like Dante's *Divina Commedia* or Milton's *Paradise Lost*. That kind of inspiration is easily detectable in many works, Christian and non-Christian, secular and religious, and it can readily be allowed to apply to parts of the Bible. But biblical inspiration has always meant more than this. It has always denoted a special endowment by God either of the author or of the text unlike any other; and of all the text, not just part of it. It is on this ground that we must reject the commonly held idea that the scriptures are inspired because they are inspiring; because they inspire us with faith and love and hope. This was the main burden of one of the earliest Anglican works which attempted to deal with the bearing of historical criticism on the inspiration of the Bible, William Sanday's *Inspiration* (1893). The argument has been advanced many times since by others. The flaw in this argument is that it does not establish the unique authority of the Bible and does not apply to the whole Bible but only to parts of it. We can readily grant the inspiring qualities of the first and fortieth chapters of Isaiah, of many Psalms, of much of the Minor Prophets, of the speeches of Job in his book, perhaps even of the stories of David's killing of Goliath, of Nathan's rebuke to David, and of many other passages in the Old Testament. And we can without difficulty find the greater part of the New Testament inspiring. But there are many passages in the Old Testament which cannot under any view be called inspiring. The story of the device of Simeon and Levi whereby they carried off Dinah (Gen. 34) is far from inspiring; it is not even edifying, except as a horrible example of how not to behave. The tale of Tamar's trick in order to obtain a husband (Genesis 38) is equally uninspiring. We could point to some passages which are to our modern ears positively indecent (e.g. Ezek. 23.17–21), and to many more, such as lists of villages in Joshua 19–21 and of names in Ezra 2 and Nehemiah 7 and 12, which nobody could call inspiring except by the most subjective of judgments. And a very large proportion of the books of Numbers, Leviticus and Deuteronomy is so much occupied with the details of the sacrificial cult now completely obsolete, that to apply the word 'inspiring' to it would be meaningless. Even the New Testament is not inspiring on every page. The Second Epistle of Peter might well strike the unprejudiced reader as a blustering piece of crude propaganda. A vindictive spirit can be detected in some parts of the Revelation (as it can in several Psalms or parts of Psalms). And from time to time there sounds beneath the prose of the New Testament a note of anti-Semitism which is anything but inspiring.

Again, we could point to other literature, Christian or secular, which is in places quite as inspiring as the Bible. Plato's *Phaedo*, Andromache's lament in Euripides' *Trojan Women*, some of the choruses in Aeschylus' *Agamemnon*, several passages in Vergil's *Aeneid* and some in Lucretius and Horace and Ovid have been found inspiring by many through the ages. All the ancients and many of the

early Christian writers were greatly inspired by Homer's epic poems.
If we were to give a list of inspiring Christian books, beginning with
Augustine's *Confessions*, *The Imitation of Christ* of Thomas à Kempis
and John Bunyan's *Pilgrim's Progress*, we would never end. The same
objection that the theory only establishes a relative and partial form of
inspiration applies to the attempt made by the Anglican, Austin
Farrer, in his *Glass of Vision* (1948). He suggested that it was the
images used by the biblical writers which were inspired, and, as in all
his books, he argued persuasively and sweetly. But other books beside
the Bible use just the same images: I Enoch, all the literature of the
Dead Sea Scrolls, early Christian and late Jewish apocalyptic works,
to mention only some. Are all these inspired too? And of course there
are books in the Bible which do not use the images used by the other
books; Job, Jonah, Proverbs, the Epistle of James. Are we to
pronounce these uninspired? In short, the argument that the Bible is
inspired because it is inspiring is not only incapable of accounting for
the whole of scripture. It is also fatally subjective. One person may
find parts inspiring which do not inspire others.

Inerrancy and inspiration have always, till recent times, been
inseparably connected. And till very recent times, as we have already
noted, inspiration, whatever it is, has always been thought to apply to
the whole Bible. 'Nowhere shall we find', says Gaussens, 'a single
passage that permits us to detach one single part of it as less divine
than the rest. When we say that this whole book is the Word of God,
do we not attest that the very phrases of which it is composed have
been given by him?'* The idea which combined inspiration and
inerrancy originally arose during the period when the Jews, returned
from exile, had concentrated their religious life round the cult of the
Temple and the keeping of the Law, and were engaged in canonizing,
preserving and studying the documents which illustrated the history
of their race. This was the period when the idea of Holy Scripture
began to establish itself. Inspiration arose as a doctrine of the schools
which studies the Torah and which set themselves to make it relevant
to the Jewish society of their day, a society which was very different
from the life of the semi-nomads of the Fertile Crescent and from the
almost wholly agricultural condition of the people whom the Hebrews
first encountered when they entered Palestine and whose way of life
they adopted. The concept of inspired writings and inspired men was
probably borrowed from the Hellenistic culture which surrounded
the Jews of the post-exilic period and which to some extent penetrated

*i.e. the Word, L. Gaussens, *Theopneustia*, Grand Rapids 1971, p. 67.

their own culture. The device of allegorizing was certainly borrowed from this source. The shamanist, ecstatic character (Saul among the prophets) and the divine oracle (the witch of Endor) appear in the Old Testament, but they are not approved of.

The primitive church took over uncritically from inter-testamental Judaism the concept of an inspired book or library of books, and the ancient church developed and enlarged it. The scriptural commentators of the first five centuries were greatly influenced by Philo, who in his voluminous works had combined the Jewish practice of allegory and the use of allegory by Hellenistic literary critics to a fantastic extent. For him the Greek version of the Hebrew scriptures (not the Septuagint but another version or versions) was quite as much inspired as the original Hebrew scriptures. The great Christian exploiter of allegory in the Philonic mode was Origen (186–255) whose many writings had an immense impact upon later Christian theologians. Although after his death Origen was generally thought to have gone too far in the use of allegory, the vast majority of Patristic and mediaeval theologians regularly used this seductive but arbitrary device in order to defend the doctrine of the verbal inspiration and inerrancy of scripture. They for the most part recognized that the Bible contained statements which were incorrect, that there were many contradictions to be found in its pages, and some things which were, on the face of it, unworthy of God or indecent or impossible. But they could dispose of these by saying that they were not meant to be taken literally, but symbolically. There was, indeed, some attempt made to harmonize apparent contradictions in the gospels especially. Augustine had declared that these contradictions could all be explained away, 'either because the manuscript is corrupt, or the translator made a mistake, or you do not understand the passage'.* And he wrote a short and unconvincing book called *The Agreement of the Four Evangelists*. But on the whole neither antiquity nor the Middle Ages were troubled by the defects or contradictions of scripture, nor did they see any serious difficulty in believing in its full inspiration and inerrancy.

The immense emphasis which the Reformation placed upon scripture was damaging to the allegorical interpretation of it, though the headings at the top of the pages of the translation of the Song of Songs in the King James Version should cure anyone of thinking that the Reformers completely abandoned allegory. Still, the more serious

---

**Epp.* 82, quoted in J. T. Burtchaell, *Catholic Theories of Inspiration since 1810*, Cambridge 1969, p. 131.

and careful attention which the scholars of the Reformation gave to the Bible resulted in the gradual rise of historical criticism of its text. And this was ultimately fatal to the use of allegory, which has now been universally rejected, except in circles which indulge in pure religious nostalgia. The upholders of the full inspiration and inerrancy of the Bible, however, were in a much more difficult situation when they had thrown away the weapon of allegory. Maintaining the inerrancy of the text in the face of historical criticism was a task of Herculean difficulty, as the next chapter will demonstrate. Even Gaussens, faced with nothing as severe as modern biblical criticism, is compelled to resort to some ludicrously complicated explanations: the quotation of Zechariah 11.12–13 erroneously ascribed to Jeremiah in Matthew 27.9–10 is a prime example: a book, Gaussens conjectures, which of course is not extant, written by Zechariah had quoted some authentic actual words of Jeremiah, just as Jude (verses 14 and 15) quotes the authentic actual words of Enoch!* Fundamentalism is dedicated to accomplishing the impossible in the field of historical criticism, and is a modern phenomenon, parasitic on the rise of criticism and existing only in reaction to it.

Finally, we must consider the arguments in favour of inspiration and inerrancy to be found summarized in Burtchaell's *Catholic Theories of Biblical Inspiration*. This illuminating book, written in a liberal and open-minded spirit, is an outstandingly useful contribution to the subject. The author reveals that ever since the beginning of the nineteenth century, Roman Catholic authors have been wrestling with the problem which the subject presents. They have taken it more seriously than Protestant theologians because for Roman Catholics the inerrancy and inspiration of the Bible is not just a time honoured doctrine handed down by tradition, but an official dogma of the church. Burtchaell traces all the vagaries of the doctrine since 1810 as the tide of opinion flowed now in the direction of a wider, and now towards the stricter definition of the terms 'inspiration' and 'inerrancy'. One may say that, generally speaking, the experts in biblical scholarship tended towards a more liberal interpretation, because they realized, at close quarters so to speak, the limitations and historical conditioning of the text. But the hierarchs and dogmatic theologians inclined to define the two concepts more strictly and literally because they wanted to preserve the traditional shape of the dogma and the reputation of the church for consistency. Both sets of theologians found it impossible to arrive at a clear and satisfactory formulation of either doctrine.

Theopneustia, pp. 216–18.

Two observations arise out of a consideration of Burtchaell's study. One is that there is a constant danger of sacrificing the normative character of the Bible in attempting to define its function. Burtchaell points out, for instance, that the theories of the Tübingen school precluded the Bible being treated as 'an exclusive norm and standard of Christian belief'.* The same tendency to regard the Bible as a launching pad rather than as a constant norm shows itself, we may remark, in Newman's *Development of Christian Doctrine*. One or two verses, a sentence here or there, will sometimes suffice for him to declare that the doctrine is scriptural, that is that somehow its faintest beginnings can be obscurely and scantily traced in scripture. But it was from the time of the ancient church and has ever been an undeviating tradition that the Bible is the norm, the standard, not merely the distant starting point, for Christian doctrine.

The other observation is, how unsatisfactory is the suggestion that inspiration applies not to the text as such but to the authors of the text. This is an argument which has been advanced again and again by writers of all complexions, and is equally vulnerable in all. In Roman Catholic writers it takes the form of claiming that the author of the biblical text was filled with or assisted or inspired by a special grace which was absent from anything else he may have written and which has been possessed by no other authors. We may as well choose this form in which to consider it. Its chief defect is that it ignores the casual or contingent nature of much of the material in the Bible. What was the grace or '*charism*' that made the author of the Pastoral Epistles refer to a cloak and parchments which he had left in Troas (II Tim. 4.13)? When St Paul wrote Second Corinthians he did not sit down to compose a careful and considered treatise (as he did when he wrote Romans). In this case he dashed off a letter in the heat of the moment, dealing with points raised by the behaviour of the Corinthians as each subject occurred to him, so that we find it difficult to reconstruct the situation, and feel when we read the letter as if we were listening to only one half of a conversation on the telephone.

What was it, we may ask, that switched on the '*charism*' so that if he had written to Timothy saying that he would meet him in three days' time bringing the cabbages with him, this would have been inspired scripture? And what was the '*charism*' of the unknown author of Psalm 137 when he wrote (verses 8 and 9): 'O daughter of Babylon . . . Happy shall he be who requites you what you have done to us. Happy shall he be who takes your little ones and dashes them

*Catholic Theories of Biblical Inspiration, p. 43.

against the rock.'? What sort of '*charism*' did the writer of the ninth chapter of the Book of Esther enjoy when he wrote the (wholly fictitious) account of Jews massacring more than 75,000 Persians, and wrote it with obvious relish? This is a passage which is never read out in church or synagogue, but which is certainly part of the Bible. We must in the end reject the idea that it is the author and not the text which is inspired, because it is an unrealistic theory produced by theologians who were not in close contact with the scriptural text itself.

At the end of this book Burtchaell gives his own views about inerrancy. He is commendably aware of the difficulty of retaining any doctrine of inerrancy. He copes with the problem in effect by so defining inerrancy that it ceases to be inerrant. 'But if inerrancy involve wild, and sometimes even frightening, movement, if it mean being pulled to the right and to the left, being tempted constantly to deviate, yet always managing somehow to regain the road, then it begins to sound like what the Church has been about.' And another definition runs thus: 'Inerrancy must be the ability, not to avoid all mistakes, but to cope with them, remedy them, survive them, and ultimately even to profit by them.'★ When is inerrancy not inerrant? Inerrancy has always meant, and, if we are not to play about irresponsibly with the meaning of words, always will mean, precisely the capacity to avoid all mistakes. All that Burtchaell is saying appears to come to this, that by and large when the final balance is taken, the Bible witnesses to truth, and this is a sentiment with which we can all agree. But this is not inerrancy, and if inerrancy is forfeited then inspiration must inevitably be forfeited too.

The fact is that both inerrancy and inspiration are categories which simply do not apply when we attach them to the Bible. They obscure rather than illuminate what the Bible has to tell us about God's dealing with men and women. They are well intentioned compliments paid to the scriptures from a very early period. They may have served for a time in God's providence to maintain the scriptures in existence. But, like some other compliments, it is better to dispense with them and to seek for other categories to explain the place which the Bible must occupy in the Christian dispensation.

★*Catholic Theories of Inspiration*, pp. 229 and 303.

Chapter Six

The Fundamentalist Interpretation

We use the name 'fundamentalism' as a useful general term to denote the theory that the Bible is inerrant. The name derives from a series of booklets called 'The Fundamentals' published in the USA between 1910 and 1915 in which, among other things, the inerrancy of the Bible was claimed to be a fundamental Christian belief. They were written by well-known evangelical theologians including Warfield, James Orr, Bishop H. C. G. Moule and G. Campbell Morgan. Those who maintain the inerrancy of the Bible do not always like being called 'fundamentalists'. They prefer the name 'Conservative Evangelicals'. But one can be a Conservative Evangelical without holding the inerrancy of the Bible and *vice versa*, so we will continue to use the term as a convenient way of referring to those who hold this view.

I

At first sight the inerrancy of the Bible would seem to be an appropriate belief for Christians to hold. Indeed those who are not believers often assume that all Christians must believe in the inerrancy of the Bible, and sometimes they give one the impression that if clergy do not hold this belief they are somehow not playing the game. Again, as we have seen, the writers of the New Testament certainly believed in the inerrancy of the Old Testament, which constituted for them the scriptures. The Christian Fathers and the mediaeval tradition continued this belief, and the Reformation did nothing to weaken it. On the contrary, since for many reformed theologians the authority of the Bible took the place which the Pope had held in the mediaeval scheme of things, the inerrancy of the Bible came to be more firmly maintained and explicitly defined among some reformed theologians than it had ever been before. Only since the very end of the seventeenth century, with the rise of biblical criticism, has this belief

in the inerrancy of the Bible been widely challenged among Christians. Why is it, then, that the inerrancy of the Bible should not be
defended by thinking Christians today?

The primary reason, from which all other reasons derive, is that
errors have been found in the Bible. Quite apart from the question of
doctrinal error, mistakes of fact occur in both the Old Testament and
the New. We will give five examples, three of which come from the
Old Testament and two from the New Testament. It must be
emphasized, however, that these are only a few examples out of very
many that could be quoted.

1. In Joshua 8.25 it is clearly stated that twelve thousand people
were slaughtered by the Israelites at Ai. Archaeological evidence has
shown that the Ai contemporary with Joshua was a small place and
could not possibly have held so many people. R. K. Harrison in his
book *Old Testament Times* writes: 'the description of the assault and
capture of a city whose population numbered twelve thousand
(Joshua 8.25) probably refers to the destruction of neighbouring
Bethel rather than Ai.'* Harrison is a fundamentalist, so he tries to
save the credit of the account by assuming that it refers to Bethel and
not Ai. But there is no justification for this in the text, which plainly
means us to understand that Ai is being referred to. Honesty compels
us to admit that here is an historical mistake.

2. In I Samuel 17.49–50 David is described as killing the Philistine
Goliath in single combat. But in II Samuel 21.19 we read 'Elhanan the
son of Jaareorgim, the Bethlemite, slew Goliath the Gittite, the shaft
of whose spear was like a weaver's beam'. Here is a blatant
inconsistency, so much so that the author of I Chronicles, writing
probably four hundred and fifty years after the event, says 'Elhanan
the son of Jair slew Lahmi the brother of Goliath the Gittite' (I Chron.
20.5). This does nothing to remove the inconsistency, but shows that
the author of Chronicles was as anxious as any fundamentalist to
preserve the inerrancy of what by his time had come to be regarded as
Holy Writ.

3. In Daniel 5.30–31 it is stated that Belshazzar the last king of
Babylon was slain by Darius the Mede and we learn in the subsequent
chapter that Darius proceeded to rule over the Babylonian empire.
Contemporary records claim that it was Cyrus who conquered
Babylon in 538 BC, and it was not until 522 that Darius succeeded to
the throne of the Persian Empire. This is confirmed by Herodotus, a
Greek historian, writing in the fifth century BC. Moreover, in Isaiah

*R. K. Harrison, *Old Testament Times*, Michigan 1970, p. 176.

44.28 and 45.1 Cyrus is referred to as the future conqueror of Babylon. Though the author of these chapters does not describe the victory of Cyrus over Babylon, he certainly expected it, and indeed attributes it to God's providential care for Israel. If ever there was an example of an historical error this passage in Daniel provides it.

4. In Mark 2.25 Jesus is defending his action in allowing his disciples to pluck corn on the sabbath by the example of David, who came to Nob and took the sacred bread in the shrine 'when Abiathar was high priest'. But if we refer to the narrative of this event in I Samuel 21.1–6 we find that the high priest was not Abiathar but Ahimelech. Matthew 12.1–8, in reproducing the story from Mark, leaves out the name of the high priest, as does Luke in Luke 6.1–5. Whether the mistake was made by Jesus himself or by Mark or by the source from which Mark drew the incident, a mistake it certainly is.

5. In Matthew 27.9–10 a passage from scripture is quoted in order to show that the burial of Judas in the potter's field was a fulfilment of prophecy. The passage is attributed by Matthew to the prophet Jeremiah, but in fact it occurs in Zechariah 11.12–13. This is no doubt a mistake on the part of the evangelist, one very easy to make since in the ancient world they did not have the benefit of the division of the books of scripture into chapters and verses that we have. Verifying a reference might be a long and difficult task. Nevertheless here is undoubtedly a mistake in the New Testament itself.

Fundamentalists of course have expended unending ingenuity in attempting to explain away these mistakes. The most common method is to put forward a series of conjectures, for which there is usually no justification in the text, which if they were true would prove that the alleged mistake was not really a mistake at all. Thus, for example, in the case of the claim in Daniel that Darius and not Cyrus captured Babylon, they have suggested that an otherwise unknown person called Darius actually preceded Cyrus. Belshazzar, again, though not actually king of Babylon when it fell, had been given quasi-regal powers by his father Nabonidus (who was in fact the last king of Babylon), and so on. Another good example occurs in Joshua 10.12–14, where according to the biblical narrative the sun 'stayed in the midst of heaven' and delayed his setting in order to enable Joshua to overthrow his enemies. We know that this could not have happened. If it had, the earth would have flown out of orbit and all life on our planet would have been extinguished. Fundamentalists therefore are driven to produce a whole series of conjectures in order to avoid the obvious conclusion that this miracle did not actually happen but is a piece of folk-legend. Thus they suggest that Joshua's attack actually took place at night and that the dawn after the night was obscured by a hailstorm, thus giving the impression that the sun had delayed in his course. There is no evidence for anything of the sort. The simplest explanation is the one we have given. A similar difficulty occurs in Numbers 1.46 where the total of fighting men during the period of the desert wandering is said to be 603,550. This is an impossibly large number. If you add the women and children who must have accompanied them you have the spectacle of well over a million people wandering around the desert of Sinai for forty years, which is quite incredible. Fundamentalists admit this and try to reduce the number to credible proportions by emending the Hebrew text. They thus save the credit of the narrative by abandoning the accuracy of the text. There is no textual evidence for this in the Hebrew of Numbers 1.46, but somehow or other inerrancy has to be defended, even at the cost of accepting the most improbable explanations.

Indeed it is the question of historical probability that is at issue here. B. B. Warfield, the great American intellectual champion of biblical inerrancy, writing towards the end of the last century, at a time when most of the difficulties of the inerrancy theory had been widely discussed, makes the following claim: 'No single error has as yet been demonstrated to occur in the Scriptures as given by God to His Church'.* To this we must reply: it depends what you mean by 'demonstrated'. It is always possible to bring forward some conjecture or other by which the admission of error can be avoided. But almost invariably the conjectures put forward are unconvincing unless one starts from the assumption that the scriptures must be inerrant. Sometimes the suggestions made in order to defend inerrancy are positively absurd. For instance one champion of inerrancy maintained that God created a special fish to swallow Jonah and a special star to guide the magi. Historical judgment is always a matter of weighing probabilities. In matters of history mathematical certainty is not to be had. But probability, often strong probability, is normally within our reach. Warfield's claim amounts to no more than this: 'No single error has yet been found in the Scriptures which cannot be explained away by the exercise of the inventive imagination and the acceptance of the most improbable conjectures.'

We can find a good parallel in the relation of the Ptolemaic to the

*B. B. Warfield, *The Inspiration and Authority of the Bible*, reissued London 1951, edited by C. van Til, p. 225.

Copernican system of astronomy. Until the heliocentric theory of the relation of the earth to the sun was put forward by Copernicus early in the sixteenth century, the Ptolemaic system was the accepted one in mediaeval Europe. Ptolemy was an astronomer of the second century AD who had worked out an explanation of the motion of the sun and the stars in relation to the earth based on a geocentric assumption. This encountered great difficulties when Ptolemy had to explain the behaviour of the planets. They do not appear to go round the earth as the sun and the moon do. So Ptolemy assumed the existence of a series of epicycles according to which the planets do indeed circle round the earth, but while doing so they complete additional circles of their own which he called epicycles; hence the appearance of irregularity. Ptolemy was thus able to account for all the known phenomena, though at the cost of constructing a very complicated system. The great merit of Copernicus' theory was that it accounted for all the phenomena in a much simpler way. When in the period after Copernicus further inventions such as the telescope produced more facts, Copernicus' explanation was vindicated. It would theoretically have been possible to account for the new phenomena on the old Ptolemaic system if astronomers had been willing to accept an even more complicated theory than that of the epicycles. But the more complicated the theory, the more improbable it became. Astronomers quite reasonably preferred the explanation that was simpler and that accounted for all of the phenomena, even though it meant abandoning a theory which had held the field for nearly a millennium and a half.

So with fundamentalist attempts to explain away errors in scripture. We cannot say that their theories are positively wrong. Rather they are improbable and often unnecessarily complicated. They are motivated not primarily by a desire to explain the facts but by an *a priori* conviction that scripture can contain no error, and therefore any theory, no matter how complicated and improbable, must be accepted rather than admit an error in scripture. The simplest, the most convincing, and the most intellectually honest course is to admit that scripture does contain errors and to be willing to face the consequences.

II

One of the arguments most often and most emphatically repeated by the defenders of the inerrancy of the Bible (it is indeed Warfield's fundamental principle) is that the Bible itself witnesses to its own inerrancy. In order to prove that the Bible is free from errors it is not enough to show that it claims to be free of errors. Let us examine the texts which are quoted in proof of this.

II Timothy 3.16–17: 'All scripture is inspired by God and profitable for teaching.' This, the RSV translation, is unsatisfactory. The phrase in Greek cannot mean 'all scripture'. It must mean 'every passage of scripture'. The author of II Timothy (in all probability not Paul but someone writing forty or fifty years after Paul's death) seems to be arguing against some people who were eclectic in their use of scripture. They only accepted some parts of scripture as inspired. The author insists that every passage in the scriptures is inspired and capable of being used in teaching. We must bear in mind however that the author can only have the Old Testament in mind. When these lines were written no part of what we now know as the New Testament would have as yet been recognized by Christians as scripture. This verse does not explicitly claim that every passage of scripture is inerrant, but in all probability the notion of inspiration would carry with it the implication of inerrancy.

I Peter 1.10–12: 'The prophets who prophesied of the grace that was to be yours searched and inquired about this salvation; they inquired what person or time was indicated by the Spirit of Christ within them when predicting the sufferings of Christ and the subsequent glory. It was revealed to them that they were serving not themselves but you in the things which have now been announced to you by those who preached the good news to you.' The author of this passage represents the Old Testament prophets as having been so much the mouthpieces of the Holy Spirit that they did not fully understand their own message. It was intended not for their own times but for the time when the Messiah should have come, i.e. the Christian era. We shall see when we come to discuss the subject of prophecy that this is a most misleading account of what the prophets were doing. Though their words often had a significance that transcended their own times, their message was always first and foremost God's word for their own contemporaries. This passage therefore proves too much. It implies a theory of inspiration of scripture which does not leave enough room for the free play of the writers' own will and mind.

II Peter 1.20–21: 'No prophecy of scripture is a matter of one's own interpretation, because no prophecy ever came by the impulse of man, but men moved by the Holy Spirit spoke from God.' The author of this passage is certainly not St Peter but someone writing in the first half of the second century. He has been troubled by heretics who gave their own peculiar interpretation of scripture. He is talking of prophecy, so he can hardly have anything more than the Old Testament in mind, though it is likely that some parts of the New Testament were regarded as scripture by the time he wrote. He insists that only the traditional interpretation, that is the church's interpretation of scripture is to be allowed. This is therefore a plea on behalf of church tradition. The author certainly believes that the Old Testament prophets were inspired, but he does not explicitly claim inerrancy for them. So this passage hardly advances the argument very much.

John 10.35: '(Scripture cannot be broken).' John represents Jesus as arguing with the Jews about the meaning of Psalm 82 which he has just quoted. He claims that the prophecy contained in that psalm must be fulfilled and has in fact been fulfilled in himself. This passage carries great weight with fundamentalists because it seems to be an argument in favour of the inerrancy of scripture from Jesus himself. In fact, however, when we allow for John's peculiar technique of taking some of Jesus' teaching and recasting and developing it so as to fit it to his own christology, we must in all honesty conclude that Jesus is very unlikely to have used this psalm as a proof for his own claims. There was among the Jews of Jesus' day a belief that no prophecy uttered by the prophets of old (and they would certainly include the Psalms among the books that contained prophecies) could ever go unfulfilled. The scripture cannot be broken. This belief was held by John and is reproduced here. There is no reason to doubt that Jesus would have held it also, though he probably did not quote this psalm.

When we consider these four passages it appears that what they prove amounts to this: the New Testament writers like all devout Jews in their time believed that the Old Testament scriptures were inspired writings and that therefore they must be true. All prophecies in the Old Testament must be fulfilled ultimately. Most of them had been fulfilled in Christ. The issue of inerrancy does not explicitly appear in any of these passages, but without doubt if any writer of the New Testament had been asked whether the scriptures (i.e. the Old Testament as we know it) were inerrant, he would have answered that they were. If we in our day, for reasons which could never have occurred to the writers of the New Testament, conclude that the scriptures are not free from error, the fact that the New Testament writers believed that they were should not in itself make us change our minds. They could not have forseen the circumstances of our time any more than Ptolemy could have foreseen the circumstances that persuaded Copernicus and Galileo to adopt the heliocentric theory.

III

There are various methods which fundamentalists use to explain apparent mistakes or inconsistencies in scripture. Of these the most frequently used perhaps is harmonizing: if we have two or more accounts of the same incident or set of incidents, they must be harmonized so as to leave no inconsistencies in scripture. The most obvious area for the exercise of harmonizing is the gospels. Thus many fundamentalists are ready to accept two cleansings of the Temple, and even two ascensions, in order to reconcile John's account with that of the synoptics.

But scripture also has to be reconciled with historical evidence from other sources if this is to be had. One obvious difficulty in this respect occurs in connection with the lineages and ages of the patriarchs in Genesis. The number of generations and the exact years of each patriarch's age must be accepted as literal fact. But neither reckoning will square with the actual age of mankind as we now know it. The writers of Genesis had no idea of the immense lapse of time that it took for *homo sapiens* to appear. Now fundamentalists do not want unnecessarily to disagree with the findings of palaeontologists and archaeologists. They are therefore compelled to assume that there are very large gaps in the genealogies from the time of Adam, gaps about which nothing at all is said in the text of the Bible. So once more we find Ptolemy-style conjectures being brought in order to preserve the inerrancy of scripture. The simplest explanation is that neither the genealogies nor the ages assigned to the patriarchs are historical in any sense. They are the work of scribes who were concerned to present the traditional legends and folk tales of Israel in a way that would form a continuous narrative from the beginning of time as they understood it. To treat them as if they were providing serious historical material is completely to misunderstand them.

There is in fact no room for legend in the fundamentalist's scheme of things. This does not mean that fundamentalists insist that there must have been a real historical prodigal son or an historical Samaritan who was travelling on the Jerusalem-Jericho road. Some fundamentalists might even be willing to admit that Job is a literary and not an historical character, though this would probably be viewed by the stricter sort as a dangerous concession to biblical criticism. But where the Bible offers what appears to be intended as a straightfoward narrative it must be accepted as history. There was, they maintain, a real Abraham who took his son Isaac to an actual mountain called Moriah in order to sacrifice him (Gen. 22.1–9). There was an historical character called Jacob who wrestled with an angel at the Jabbok (Gen. 32.22–32). God did actually command that the man who gathered sticks on the sabbath day should be stoned to death (Num. 15.32–36). Korah, Dathan and Abiram with their entire families were actually swallowed up by the earth because they rebelled against Moses and Aaron (Num. 16.1–40), and so on.

There does not seem to be very much room for myth either. There are places where some Old Testament writers refer to traditional myths, for example in Isaiah 27.1 we have a reference to 'Leviathan the fleeing serpent', and we learn that God will 'slay the dragon that is in the sea'. And in Isaiah 51.9 the prophet exclaims 'Was it not thou (the arm of the Lord) that didst cut Rahab in pieces, that didst pierce the dragon?' R. K. Harrison* admits that Leviathan and Rahab are mythological, but claims that they are only used as poetic embellishment, similar to Milton's use of pagan mythology in *Paradise Lost*. We are dealing of course with two prophets here. One was Isaiah of Jerusalem, who flourished about 700 BC. The other lived a century and a half later during the Babylonian exile. But if one studies both passages honestly one can only conclude that both prophets believed in God's victory over the chaos dragon as firmly as they believed in his deliverance of his people from Egypt.

Indeed one of the great difficulties encountered by the fundamentalist is that of deciding when to interpret the Bible literally and when metaphorically. He would normally prefer to understand it literally; as we have seen, whenever he can he accepts narrative as straightforward history, even when it appears to have been written hundreds of years after the event, as is the case with the Books of Chronicles. But there are passages in which the literal sense simply will not do for someone who wishes to preserve the inerrancy of the Bible. Exodus 4.24–26 is surely such a passage. Even the most fervent advocate of the literal truth of the Bible would hesitate to accept the conclusion that the God revealed to us in Jesus Christ required to be appeased by the offering of Gershom's foreskin. It is therefore inaccurate to say that fundamentalists are literalists. It might be more satisfactory to claim that they are literalists unless they meet something in the Bible that seems to be too anthropomorphic or primitive or offensive to

Old Testament Times, p. 166.

Christian standards of morality. When this happens they propose a non-literal interpretation.

Another point of great importance to fundamentalists is that in any passage where Jesus seems to have accepted the literal truth or the traditional authorship of a passage or book in the Old Testament, that decision must be accepted as inerrant. Jesus' authority on these matters is infallible and must not be questioned. For instance in Mark 12.35–37 (parallels Matt. 22.41–46; Luke 20.41–44) Jesus accepts the Davidic authorship of Psalm 110. Again in Matthew 12.39f.; 16.4; Luke 11.16f. Jesus refers to the sign of the prophet Jonah and to his having been three days in the belly of the whale. The fundamentalist uses this as an argument in defence of the completely historical nature of the tale of Jonah. Likewise Matthew 24.15 is seen as a proof that Daniel is one of the prophetic books. The suggestion that Jesus, because he was truly man, was bound by the intellectual presuppositions of the age and place in which he was born would not find favour with fundamentalists.

There is in fact a strong element of positivism in the fundamentalist approach to the Bible. This is the conviction that everything must be capable of being clearly stated in black and white and if possible proved scientifically. Jesus was *either* divine and therefore infallible *or* he was an imposter. The Book of Jonah is *either* straightforward history *or* it is a fraud. The Pentateuch is *either* a reliable history of the Jews from the time of Abraham till the time of the entry into Canaan *or* it is a tissue of falsehoods. The fundamentalist has the greatest difficulty in allowing for the possibility that there is more than one way of conveying truth. Legend, myth, story, and poetry can all be used, and have been used, by the Holy Spirit to witness to God's dealings with men. We do not have to reduce them all to simple historical narrative.

There is a very similar situation when we consider the fundamentalist's view of revelation in the Bible. He is not content to say that we have in the Bible a record of God's character as reflected in the writings of those whom he inspired. The fundamentalist wants something more positive than that. He regards the Bible as first and foremost a teaching book, and he would like to be able to extract a number of fundamental doctrines from it so as to give to these doctrines the benefit of the Bible's inerrancy. Thus the fundamentalist will frequently say: 'The Bible teaches . . .', where the critical student would want to ask: 'Which part of the Bible teaches. . . ?' For the fundamentalist the Bible appears more uniform and integrated than it does to the critical scholar. For instance Cornelius van Til, the modern editor of Warfield, believes in 'propositional revelation', and he regards the Bible as a book containing 'objective truths', indeed a system of objective truths.* However, when one asks what are these truths which constitute revelation one runs into great difficulties. Is one to treat every statement in the Bible that seems to be concerned with doctrine as a revealed proposition? Or does one merely take the summaries of the Bible's messages contained in the catholic creeds as constituting the revelation? The first would seem to include far too much and the second too little. What most people who hold to a view of 'propositional revelation' and 'objective truths' do is to make their own selection of what they regard as essential revealed truths contained in the Bible; and their choice will be very much influenced by their own theological tradition. Most fundamentalists for instance would include among revealed truths some sort of a statement defining a penal substitutionary doctrine of the atonement.

IV

There are still some characteristics of the Bible itself we have to mention which cause difficulty to fundamentalists but not to the student who is willing to accept the critical approach. The first is this: the fundamentalist believes that the Bible is inerrant. But can he be sure that we have the original text of the Bible? In parts of both the Old Testament and the New there are alternative readings in the oldest manuscripts. There are some places where it may be impossible to say with certainty what the original text was. This is much more frequent in the Old Testament, but there may be some such passages in the New Testament, e.g. John 8.25. This only presents a problem to those who hold that the Bible is inerrant, and fundamentalists are divided as to how to cope with it. Sometimes they maintain that the text as we now have it, handed down through so many centuries, is not the inerrant one. The trouble with this solution is that it deprives the fundamentalist of his inerrant Bible; only the original was inerrant. For all we know the text we now have may be full of errors. A more common method is to play down the differences in the oldest texts and to suggest that what we have is virtually the autograph, the text as it was when it left the writer's pen. Thus van Til, writing about the efforts of what he calls orthodox (i.e. fundamentalist) scholars to

The Inspiration and Authority of the Bible, pp. 30 and 38.

recover the original text, says: 'They have every right to believe that they are on the right road and that the end of their way is near at hand.'* If this means that they are within an ace of recovering the original text of the entire Bible, it is a madly optimistic forecast. In any case, how do they know that they are using the right methods? How can they recognize the original text when they have found it? They do not claim to be inerrant. How can a lost inerrant text be recovered by scholars who are not themselves inerrant?

A subsidiary difficulty is connected with the Hebrew text of the Old Testament. Until a late date in the history of the transmission of the text, about the fourth century AD, the Hebrew text was written without any vowels being indicated such as we find in most Hebrew Bibles today. This absence of vowels during a period of transmission lasting so many centuries left room for a very wide possibility of error in trans-scribing; and in fact in a great many places where there is doubt about the reading of the original Hebrew the doubt concerns the vocalization of the text. One has only to look at a critical text of the Hebrew, such as R. Kittel's *Biblia Hebraica*, to see how often on almost any page the margin contains conjectures and alternative readings. Where there are obscure books such as Job, or obscure passages such as Isaiah 53, the number of places where the Hebrew needs emendation is immense. To suggest that the original text of the Hebrew Old Testament could have reached us almost intact under such conditions of transmission is absurd. An inerrant Bible requires an inerrant text, and that we have not got.

Thirdly, New Testament writers very frequently quote the Old Testament. If, for example, one reads the Greek New Testament in the Bible Societies' edition of 1966, one can observe how often the Greek is printed in bold type, indicating a quotation for the Old Testament. But New Testament writers do not by any means reproduce the Old Testament as we have it. They are quoting in Greek, of course, so one would expect them to reproduce the LXX, the Septuagint, the official Greek translation made from about 250 BC onwards. Very often, however, they do not quote the LXX version but produce their own translation, whether translating directly from the Hebrew or using another Greek translation. A good example is Isaiah 6.9–10, a passage in which God predicts that Israel would be blind to the prophet's message. This is a popular quotation with New Testament writers: it is quoted in Matthew 13.14–15; Mark 4.12; Luke 8.10; Acts 28.26–27, and John 12.40. But they all seem to quote

**The Inspiration and Authority of the Bible*, p. 46.

a different version of it. Matthew does not agree with Mark. Luke rather inclines to an abbreviated form of Mark's version. But in Acts 28.26–27 he has what is virtually Matthew's version. And John has his own version which does not exactly agree with any of the others. None of them can be said to be an exact rendering of the Hebrew. Now all these versions cannot together be inerrant; some of them must be less accurate than the others. All the writers presumably believe that they are reproducing what the prophet originally said, but they cannot all be inerrantly right.

There is a further complication here. There are some passages in the New Testament where the writer quotes the LXX in order to make a doctrinal point of some importance. But the LXX in these passages has mistranslated the Hebrew. A clear example is Matthew 1.23, where Isaiah 7.14 is quoted in the form 'A virgin shall conceive and bear a son'. But the LXX has not translated the Hebrew accurately. The Hebrew word translated 'virgin' only means 'a young woman' and in fact what the prophet is saying is that a young (married) woman will conceive and bear a son. The LXX text has imported the idea of a virgin into the text. Matthew gladly takes it up, regarding it as a prophecy of Jesus' birth from a virgin. Another example occurs in Hebrews 10.5, where the author quotes Psalm 40.6 in its LXX version. This runs:

> Sacrifice and offering thou hast not required,
> but a body thou hast prepared for me.

The author of Hebrews, who shows no signs of any acquaintance with Hebrew, readily accepts the LXX translation as a prophecy of the incarnation. In fact, however, the LXX has mistranslated the Hebrew. It is true indeed that the Hebrew is obscure. The RSV renders:

> Sacrifice and offering thou dost not desire,
> but thou hast given me an open ear.

This may not be the original meaning; the experts do not agree. But nobody suggests that 'a body thou has prepared for me' correctly represents the original meaning of the Hebrew, and it is not clear by what route the LXX translator achieved this mistranslation. Passages such as these in the New Testament raise formidable problems for the fundamentalist which do not trouble the critical student.

We will give one more example of the fundamentalist creating problems for himself. We have had occasion to refer already to R. K. Harrison's book *Old Testament Times*. It is a survey of the history of Israel as recorded in the Old Testament. Harrison is well read in the literature of the Old Testament and within the limits of his fundamentalist presuppositions gives a reasonable account of the Old Testament background. But there are places where his fundamentalism actually inhibits him from using all the historical evidence that exists. An instance of this occurs in his account of Israel during the Babylonian exile. One of our main contemporary historical sources for this period is the work of the anonymous prophet of the exile whose prophecies are to be found in chapters 40–55 of the Book of Isaiah. If we scan these chapters carefully we can learn quite a lot about the condition of those whom the prophet was addressing. But Harrison is inhibited from using this evidence because he does not accept the theory universally held by all non-fundamentalist scholars, that chapters 40–55 of the Book of Isaiah belong to the period of the exile. The remarkable consequence is that R. K. Harrison nowhere in his book mentions these chapters. This is all the more astonishing because they contain some of the most important theological thought in the Old Testament. Is it perhaps that Harrison is not quite prepared to act on his own convictions? Presumably he holds that Isaiah of Jerusalem about the year 700 BC was superhumanly enlightened so as to be able to foresee the events of the history of his people some one hundred and fifty years after his own time, including the name of the conqueror, Cyrus, who was to deliver them. If so, why not make use of this information in order to learn something about the condition of Israel in exile? One has only to state this theory to show its absurdity. No wonder that Harrison preserves a silence on the subject.

In 1987 a very interesting study was published written by N. M. de S. Cameron called *Biblical Higher Criticism and the Defense of Infallibilism in Nineteenth Century Britain* (New York and Queenstown Ontario). It offers a review of the controversy between the defenders of the inerrancy of the Bible and the champions of the critical approach during the second half of the last century in this country. Two conclusions seem to emerge as far as concerns fundamentalism today. The first is that it is not likely that fundamentalists will be able to produce any new arguments. All the issues for and against the inerrancy of the Bible have been explored and debated. The second conclusion is this: once the defender of the inerrancy of the Bible allows himself to meet the critic on critical grounds and not on grounds of *a priori* principle, he is lost. He finds himself involved in more and more complicated and improbable conjectures in order to save the Bible's inerrancy, and he is vulnerable at so many points, that the effort to defend every weak position becomes impossible or rather incredible. He is caught, one might say, in a Ptolemaic system of epicycles and yet more epicycles. It can hardly be a coincidence that the fundamentalist tradition has not produced one biblical commentator of sufficient status as to be recognized throughout the scholarly world. It is as if the effort to defend the inerrancy of the Bible exhausts the creative imagination – or else such an attempt does not appeal to those who possess a creative imagination. The fundamentalist interpretation of the Bible will no doubt continue to appeal to some Bible students always. But for those who have a regard for intellectual honesty it must be regarded as a lost cause.

Chapter Seven

Prophecy

In the New Testament and the early church generally prophecy meant foretelling the future. There were people called prophets in the church of the New Testament, but it is not with them that we are concerned. We have in mind the prophets of old, the prophets whose work is found in what we call the Old Testament, but what the New Testament writers knew as 'the scriptures'. They are often alluded to in the New Testament. It may even be that in Ephesians 2.20 they are coupled with the apostles as forming the foundation of the church.

There can be no doubt but that the New Testament writers regarded the prophets of old as having foretold the events connected with the coming of Christ. These prophets are frequently quoted in the New Testament, often by name. There may indeed be some variation in the New Testament as to how much the prophets knew about the future. Paul and John give us the impression that the Old Testament prophets were very well informed indeed. For example, in Romans 10.14–21 we have a passage in which Paul quotes a whole series of texts from the Old Testament designed to prove that Israel of old was given a great deal of advance information about Christ, if only they had been willing to believe it. He quotes Isaiah twice, Deuteronomy once, and the Psalms once. This would imply that according to Paul, Moses, David and Isaiah were all well informed about the future messianic era.

We should note at this point that 'the prophets' for New Testament writers included not only the canonical prophets from Isaiah to Malachi whom we have in our Old Testament, but also Moses as the supposed author of the Pentateuch and David as the supposed author of the Psalms. New Testament writers, following contemporary Jewish belief, held that Moses and David had just as much prophetic spirit as any of the canonical prophets. If we want another example of this belief in Paul's writings, we can study II Corinthians 3.7–18, where it seems to be implied that Moses put on the veil while speaking to the Israelites because he did not want them to learn about the glory of Christ which shone from his face. In other words, Moses had encountered the pre-existent Christ and knew about his future history. The same belief is found in the Fourth Gospel: see John 1.45; 5.46–47, where it is stated in so many words that Moses wrote about Jesus.

In I Peter 1.10–12, however, it is suggested that the prophets did not have full knowledge of what it was their words referred to. All they knew was that their utterances were not to find fulfilment in their own days, but in the messianic era, which of course Christians claimed had now arrived with the coming of Jesus Christ. A similar belief can be found in the writings of the Qumran Community. See 1Q Hab. 2.1–3. We can also find speculations among the Jewish exegetes of a later period as to the relative degrees of inspiration enjoyed by the prophets. It was held that Isaiah received the greatest degree of inspiration. Others such as Ezekiel were less fully inspired.

Not content with holding that the prophets of the Old Testament, including Moses and David, foretold in various ways the coming of Christ, the greatest theologians of the New Testament, Paul, John and the author of Hebrews, occasionally quoted the Psalms under the conviction that we can sometimes detect in them utterances of the pre-existent Christ, or even utterances of the Father to the pre-existent Son. A clear example of this occurs in Hebrews, chapters 1 and 2. See Hebrews 1.5, 8, 10, 13, where Psalms 2, 104, 102 and 110, as well as II Samuel 7.14 are interpreted as uttered by the Father to the pre-existent Son; and in Hebrews 2.12–13 the pre-existent Son is represented as speaking to the Father in Psalm 22.22 and Isaiah 8.17–18. But Paul uses this technique also: see Romans 15.3 where the pre-existent Christ is represented as uttering the words of Psalm 69.9 to the Father, and following them up with the words of Psalm 18.49. We can find a parallel to this in John 2.17, where John quotes Psalm 69.9 as uttered by Christ to the Father as a prophecy of his death.

It would not be quite accurate to say, as some scholars have said, that the New Testament writers lifted verses out of the scripture without any regard to their context. In fact they often pay a lot of attention to the context, but in a literary not an historical sense. They were not interested in the question: 'What did these words mean when they were originally uttered?' The question they were concerned with was: 'What do these words mean to us today, who live in the messianic era?' Very often we can learn much about what the New Testament writers thought the prophetic utterances meant if we read the whole passage from which the quotation is taken.

We come back, however, to our original statement: for the New Testament writers prophecy meant foretelling the future. They were interested in the Scriptures primarily because they believed that the scriptures were full of prophecies about Christ. This approach to the Old Testament was enthusiastically adopted by the Christian writers of the period following that of the New Testament, so that by the time we reach the fourth and fifth centuries AD, the epoch in which the basic Christian doctrine of God was formulated and agreed, it was considered legitimate to use the most far-fetched allegory and analogy in order to find prophecies of the career of Christ and of the founding of the church in every part of the Old Testament, no matter how remote its subject matter might appear to be at first sight from that with which the Christian faith was concerned.

II

Perhaps this is the point at which to define what we mean by prophecy. Prophecy means that the Holy Spirit, or the prophet himself, intended the words of the prophet to refer to the messianic era in the future and not to the prophet's own immediate circumstances. Or alternatively that the prophets uttered their words without knowing what they referred to, but the Holy Spirit intended them to refer to the messianic era. This is certainly what the New Testament writers understood by prophecy. It must follow of course that prophecy in this sense was fulfilled in the messianic era, that is, in the events connected with the career of Jesus Christ.

Prophecy understood in this sense, we maintain, did not take place. This is not to deny that there is such a thing as Old Testament prophecy fulfilled in the events concerning Jesus Christ, as we shall be indicating later on. But we deny that fulfilment took place in the way in which the New Testament writers believed it did, that is, by prophets uttering words whose sole significance lay in their fulfilment hundreds of years after they were uttered. The prophets were not primarily predictors, and they were granted no superhuman knowledge about events which were to take place in the future. We justify these claims on the following grounds.

(*a*) The Old Testament prophets certainly spoke about what was to happen in the future. But it was the immediate future and the future events were always closely connected with what was happening at the time when the prophet was speaking. They gave no detailed prophecies about events which would only happen hundreds of years later. Moreover, the prophets were given no superhuman knowledge of future events, since frequently their prophecies were not fulfilled and sometimes events turned out differently to the way in which they had said they would happen. In other words, they were not divinely inspired to predict future events. They were making conjectures and forecasts about the immediate future in the way any well-informed person might have done. The real value of their prophecies lay not in their predictive element but in something else. What that was, we shall be expounding later on.

Thus we find Jeremiah predicting a dishonoured death for king Jehoiakim. See Jeremiah 22.18–19; 36.29–31, where Jeremiah says that Jehoiakim will be given the burial of an ass. But in II Kings 24.6 the reference to the death of Jehoiakim mentions no such event. His death is recorded in exactly the same way as is the death of the other kings of Judah. Another clear example of unfulfilled prophecy occurs in Ezekiel 26.7–14; 29.17–20. In the first passage the prophet foretells the fall of Tyre at the hand of Nebuchadnezzar, king of Babylon. In the second the prophet declares that Nebuchadnezzar had not after all succeeded in taking Tyre but that God would give him Egypt instead. We should notice that in neither of these instances does the prophet seem embarrassed by the fact that his prophecy was mistaken. He makes no apology. The prophets did not regard themselves as infallible mouth-pieces of God. Nothing could be farther from the truth, therefore, than the claim made by fundamentalists that everything the prophets wrote must be regarded as the exact words of God himself. Warfield claims, for example writes: 'Jehovah put his words in the mouths of the prophets, and the prophets spoke precisely these words and no others.'* Such a belief witnesses to a hankering for direct unmediated knowledge of God such as God does not provide. We must always make allowances for the fact that God uses us humans, with all our peculiarities and weaknesses, as the means by which he addresses us; and his message never comes to us unconditioned by the human intermediary.

(*b*) In many passages in the New Testament where prophecies from the Old Testament are cited as having been fulfilled in the coming of

*Warfield, *The Inspiration and Authority of the Bible*, p. 87.

Christ a close inspection shows that the alleged prophecies were not intended as predictions of messianic events at all. When originally uttered they referred to events of the prophet's own time, or even earlier. Thus in Matthew 2.15 it is claimed that Hosea 11.1 is fulfilled in the flight into Egypt of the holy family. The words are 'Out of Egypt have I called my son'. But when we look up these words in the context of Hosea 11, we find that they do not refer to the future at all. Hosea is looking back to the past: God has called Israel his son out of bondage to serve him. It refers to God's election of the children of Israel, not to any event in the life of Jesus Christ. Similarly in Acts 13.35 in his sermon at Pisidian Antioch Paul is represented as quoting Psalm 16.10: 'Thou shalt not permit thy Holy One to see corruption.' Paul argues that these words could not have been meant to refer to David, the supposed author of all the Psalms, since it is well known that David did die and his body saw corruption. It must therefore be a prophecy of the resurrection of Jesus Christ, God's Holy One. But if we turn to Psalm 16.10 there is no suggestion in it that it has any messianic reference at all. The title of the Psalm is 'A Miktam of David', but scholars are agreed that the 'titles' of the Psalms are not an original part of the Psalms but are later guesses or pieces of traditional lore added by some scribe or scribes. The obvious conclusion is that Psalm 16.10 represents the aspiration, the hope, the act of faith of some devout believer in Israel. It is very closely akin to Jesus' own argument in favour of resurrection which we find in Mark 12.24–27: if God has made himself known to us in intimate communion during our life, he will not abandon us at death. A third example could be found in the psalm cited in Hebrews 1.10–12. It is Psalm 102.25–27. Only someone who had already made up his mind to find prophecies of Christ in the Psalms could believe that in these verses the Father is addressing the Son. The natural interpretation of this passage is to see it as the psalmist's address to God, in which he contrasts God's eternity with his own ephemeral existence.

(*c*) If it were the case that Old Testament prophets were able to foresee the events of Our Lord's life in detail because they were superhumanly endowed with a knowledge of future events, their way of declaring this is a very strange one, because when they give what is alleged to be a description of the Messiah, only some details seem to fit the life of Jesus Christ. Others are left unfulfilled. We will take two examples from what Christians have traditionally believed to be passages of messianic prophecy in the Book of Isaiah. The first is Isaiah 7.14–15. As we have seen, this passage is cited as a prophecy of the birth of Jesus in Matthew 1.23, in the form: 'a virgin shall conceive and bear a son and shall call his name Immanuel, that is "God with us".' Now the prophecy does not end there but continues: 'He shall eat curds and honey when he knows how to refuse the evil and choose the good', that is, by the time he comes to years of discretion the land will be reduced to the most dire straits, since curds and honey were apparently the iron ration, or basic minimum food to enable one to survive in time of scarcity. But of course we hear nothing about Jesus eating curds and honey. That part of the prophecy does not apply.

Next we turn to Isaiah 52.13–53.12. This is a passage of immense significance for our understanding of the relation of the Old Testament to the New, as we shall be seeing. It is frequently quoted or alluded to in the New Testament. No New Testament writer had the slightest doubt but that the mysterious 'servant of the Lord' described in this passage was indeed Jesus Christ. It seems very probable that Jesus himself found in this passage, among others, inspiration for his mission. But if we take it literally as an inspired description of the career of Jesus Christ foretold by Isaiah seven hundred years before the coming of Christ, we must confess that it does not fit him in every detail. For instance the servant is described thus in 52.11: 'his appearance was so marred beyond human semblance, and his form beyond that of the sons of men.' This seems to suggest that he was afflicted by some terrible disfiguring disease such as leprosy. But there is not hint of this in the career of Jesus. Again 53.2–3 continues thus:

> he had no form or comeliness that we should look at him,
> and no beauty that we should desire him,
> a man of pains and acquainted with sickness.

We have preferred the RSV margin rendering here, because it translates the Hebrew more accurately. The translation in the text seems to have been a little influenced by the traditional Christian interpretation of the passage. But there is no evidence that Jesus was unattractive or repulsive in appearance, nor that he was particularly prone to sickness or pain. In effect, therefore if Old Testament prophecy is understood in a literal or predictive sense, it does not always fit. If the prophets had been superhumanly endowed with knowledge of the future one might expect that they would always have got it exactly right.

(*d*) But there is a philosophical or theological difficulty about the very idea of detailed prediction. If some of the prophets were given advance detailed information about what was to happen centuries after their time, it seems to imply that all events are predetermined, and thus to do away with human freedom. This can be avoided of course by saying that God knows all the alternatives open to everyone in all conceivable circumstances; he also knows our characters, and thus knows in advance what decisions we shall make while leaving us free to make them. Nevertheless, when we come to work out the actual implications in history of a literal belief in predictive prophecy operative over periods measuring hundreds of years, the results cannot but appear disquieting. We will take two examples: in I Kings 13.1–2 we have an account of how 'a man of God' visited King Jeroboam of Israel at Bethel and prophesied that in days to come the altar on which Jeroboam was burning incense would be profaned. The prophet addresses the altar thus: 'Behold, a son shall be born to the house of David, Josiah by name; and he shall sacrifice upon you the priests of the high places.' If we now turn to II Kings 23.15–16 we can see that this prophecy was fulfilled. We are asked to believe that the 'man of God' knew the name of a future king of Judah three hundred years before he was born. Are we to imagine that Josiah's parents had read this passage and carefully consulted it before naming this new-born son? (But how did they know that he was going to fulfil this prophecy?) Or were they divinely guided to give this name to this son in order that the prophecy should be fulfilled? A theory that involved so much direct and supernatural intervention by God must make us suspicious. A much more probable explanation is that provided by the Old Testament scholars: I Kings 13 is a legend invented after the time of Josiah perhaps in order to justify his treatment of the shrine in Bethel. The 'prophecy' is a *vaticinatio post eventum*, a prophecy after the event.

A second example is equally difficult. In Isaiah 44.28; 45.1 we have two references to Cyrus. The prophet declares that he is God's anointed, raised up in order to overthrow the Babylonian Empire and allow Israel to return to its homeland and rebuild the Temple. We can date Cyrus' career very accurately, and it looks very much as if this passage describes him at the point in his career of conquest which he must have reached about the year 448 BC when he overthrew Croesus of Lydia. If we follow the traditional view of prophecy this passage was composed by the prophet Isaiah of Jerusalem, who flourished about 700 BC. He was therefore given superhuman prevision about an individual actually named who was to live a hundred and fifty years after his time. Even if we could swallow this, we might well ask, what was the point of supplying Isaiah with this pre-information? Why should he be told of someone who would have no bearing on him or on any of his contemporaries? A far simpler account of the matter is to conclude with all competent students of the Old Testament that chapters 40–55 of the Book of Isaiah were not written by Isaiah of Jerusalem about 700 BC but by an anonymous prophet who lived in Babylon during the exile, and who was therefore a contemporary of Cyrus.

Great as are the difficulties which a literal interpretation of prophecy must raise in connection with passages such as these, they are minor compared with those which are encountered in connection with the Book of Daniel. If we take it at its face value, the Book of Daniel is written partly at the end of the Babylonian Empire (which fell in 538 BC) and partly in the beginning of the Persian Empire which succeeded it. Quite half the book is taken up with apparent prophecies about the history of the next four hundred years. This culminates in chapter 11 in a detailed account of future history, concentrating particularly on the period of Greek rule from 333 BC till 165 BC. If this were authentic prophecy it would mean that Daniel was granted a great deal of detailed information about future events, including details of the relations between the Seleucid and Ptolemaic dynasties, which did not exist at the time when Daniel was supposed to be living. The situation is complicated by the fact that the 'prophecies' are not all equally accurate. The information about the fall of the Babylonian empire and the rise of the Persian empire is inaccurate in several respects. As the prophetic history comes closer to the time of Antiochus IV Epiphanes it grows more accurate. Traditional Christian scholarship right up to the time of E. B. Pusey in the last century accepted the book at its face value and regarded it as a wonderful example of superhumanly inspired prophecy. But modern scholars have refused to accept so remarkable and implausible an example of prophetic inspiration. They agree with the view put forward by the pagan scholar Porphyry in the third century AD that the book was written during the Antiochene persecution, probably between 168 and 165 BC and that the greatest part of the apparent 'prophecy' in the book is *post eventum*. The Book of Daniel is surely the graveyard of the traditional concept of predictive prophecy in the Old Testament.

(*e*) One more mistaken view of prophecy needs to be considered. There are some people who believe that by studying the Old Testament prophets, more especially Ezekiel and Daniel, we could learn something about what is to happen in our day. In other words, some of the Old Testament prophets were not only commissioned to say what was to happen at the coming of Christ, but also what was to happen more than two thousand years later on a world scale. Before the last war the most vocal of this group of believers called themselves British Israelites. They had worked out an elaborate scheme of future history based largely on Old Testament passages taken right out of their context, according to which the powers of evil represented by Germany and Russia would come to a decisive battle with the forces of goodness represented by the British Empire. The battle would take place in Palestine and would be ended by God's personal intervention. As long as Rommel was winning in North Africa the British Israelites were delighted, because events seemed to be going according to their plan – the forces of evil were advancing towards Palestine, where they were to meet their Megiddo. But the battle of El Alamein put an end to these sanguine hopes and less has been heard of the British Israelites since. But their place has been taken by a whole series of writers and religious interpreters who today make much more far-reaching claims about the way in which the Bible can be used to plot the course of future history. These include not only Christian believers, who value the Bible in itself quite apart from their belief in its predictive quality, but also quite secular-minded people who treat the Bible as if it was a reliable historical document which also possesses the unusual feature of relating future history. It is of course totally un-Christian to treat the Old Testament as if it were a magic book that can predict future history. The prophets of the Old Testament find their fulfilment in the New Testament dispensation or nowhere. There are still mis-guided people who eagerly search both Old and New Testaments for information about coming events in our own day. It is a totally fruitless activity. Indeed we have been warned against doing any such thing repeatedly in the New Testament; see Mark 13.32 (parallels are Matt. 24.36, Luke 17.20f.); II Thessalonians 2.1–3; Acts 1.7. Such an abuse of scripture must be left to fanatics, fools and semi-literates. The true Christian understanding of the fulfilment of prophecy is something much deeper and much more closely connected with the revelation of God in Jesus Christ.

III

So far we have gone to great lengths to explain what prophecy in the Old Testament is not. It is time that we turned to an explanation of what it is. In order to do this, we will examine all the important canonical prophets in order. But first, we must explain why we begin

with the canonical prophets. The New Testament writers would not
have adopted this approach: they would have begun with Moses or
even earlier; (Gen. 49.10c is probably regarded as a messianic
prophecy in John 9.7). They would also have included Baalam and
David (see Luke 24.27). Baalam seems a strange figure to appear
among the prophets, since he was represented in Jewish tradition as a
reprehensible character who tried to pervert Israel from worshipping
Jahweh. But his prophecy in Numbers 24.17 was regarded as too
valuable to forego, and so he was considered to have been the
instrument of the Holy Spirit despite his regrettable behaviour (see
Matt. 2.2; Rev. 22.16). Notice how he is described as a prophet in II
Peter 2.16. The reason we omit everyone before the canonical
prophets is that there is no genuine ground for believing that either
Moses or Baalam or David thought of themselves as prophets in the
true sense. We have in any case no writings in the Old Testament
which we can with any confidence attribute to Moses. Baalam is a
character in a folk tale and is no more historical than Robin Hood;
David, though he was probably the author of a few of the very oldest
Psalms, had no intention of prophesying about the messianic era.

We begin then with Amos, probably the earliest of the written
prophets. The essence of his message is that God is not content with
the sacrifices and celebrations which Israel offered with great
scrupulousness in his honour. He requires above all righteous
conduct, and this Israel is not manifesting. Amos denounces especially the social sins of Israel, oppression of the poor, profligacy, the
luxury of the rich, corruption in the law-courts (2.6–8; 3.10; 4.1–3;
5.10–15; 6.1–8). Because of these sins judgment will soon fall upon
the nation. It is probable that Amos himself did not foresee a time
when Israel would be restored. The last few verses of his book (9.5–
15) are probably the work of a later scribe (or scribes) who wished to
make the prophecy correspond more exactly with what actually
happened.

We turn to Hosea, who lived not long after Amos, perhaps as his
junior contemporary. Both belong to the eighth century BC, Amos
about the middle of it, Hosea a little later. Hosea condemns much the
same sins as does Amos; see Hosea 4.1–6; 6.7–10; 7.1–7; 12.7–9. But
he also denounces Israel's abandonment of Jahweh in that they have
adopted the bull-cult from the Canaanites. They are worshipping the
local gods, the baals, he says, and not their true God. However, Hosea
has a very positive message as well, one of very great significance
indeed as far as concerns Old Testament prophecy. God, he says, still

loves Israel despite her unfaithfulness. Hosea uses the analogy of his own marriage to describe God's relation to Israel. He had married a wife who bore him two children and then deserted him. Hosea went in search of her and brought her back from the man with whom she was living. So Israel has deserted God, who originally adopted her as his bride by means of the events of the exodus and desert sojourn. But God will seek her, discipline her and win her back for himself. For all this see chapter 1–3, and most of all the magnificent chapter 11, where Hosea describes in glowing terms the overwhelming love of God: he cannot abandon Israel, no matter how far she has strayed; his love constrains ..m to spare her and win her back. A study of Hosea must convince us how mistaken is the popular opinion that in the Old Testament we only meet a God of wrath, and that belief in the love of God is confined to the New Testament.

The prophet Isaiah flourished between 743 (the date of his call, see 6.1) and some time after 700 BC. He, like his predecessors, condemned the social injustice of his people. See the whole of chapter 1; also 3.16–26 (luxury of the rich); 5.8–12, 20–23 (drunkenness, luxury and social oppression); 2.6,19,20; 8.19 (idolatry and occult practices); 10.1–2 (social oppression); 28.1–8 (drunkenness again). Isaiah addressed himself solely to the southern kingdom, Judah, centred on Jerusalem where he lived. He has a profound understanding of God's righteousness and holiness (see again the account of his call in chapter 6), and has no doubt but that Judah will be punished for her sins. She like Israel in Amos' day had to be reminded that God has no use for offerings and celebrations divorced from right living. See 1.12–17. Isaiah, however, was convinced that God would never abandon Jerusalem, because his dwelling place, the Temple, stood there, and when King Hezekiah was threatened by Assyria, the prophet encouraged him to stand firm because God would not allow Zion to be profaned; see 37.21–35. We must remember that during Isaiah's life-time, in 721 BC to be precise, the northern kingdom centred on Samaria was abolished by the Assyrians, and most of its people carried away captive.

So far we have said much about the prophets but nothing about messianic prophecy. This is because there is nothing corresponding to messianic prophecy before the time of Isaiah. But in Isaiah we do find some passages such as 9.2–7; 11.1–11; 32.1–8 in which the prophet looks forward to a future golden age, when Israel will dwell securely under a king from the line of David, and all conflict and evil will have been done away with. But the word 'Messiah' (='Anointed One') is not used. Though later generations certainly regarded these passages as messianic, it might be more accurate to describe them as utopian or idealistic. Not every word in the first thirty-nine chapters of the Book of Isaiah is from the pen of the prophet; and, as we shall be seeing, nothing in the book after chapter 39 is his.

Micah also lived in the southern kingdom and was a contemporary of Isaiah, but he was a countryman, not a townsman like Isaiah. He condemns social oppression (2.1–5); corruption and mutual enmity and hatred (7.1–7). He is also remarkable for the way in which he condemns both religious and secular leaders: prophets, priests, and magistrates are all equally corrupt: 2.6–11; 3.1–12; 6.9–16. In his relatively brief prophecy of seven chapters, not all of which are from his time, Micah, the non-establishment figure, shows astonishing boldness in denouncing all the most powerful classes. There is evidence that his word did not go unheeded and that the king did not punish him for his courage – see Jeremiah 26.16–19.

Jeremiah's long ministry extended from before Josiah's reformation in 621 BC until well after the fall of Jerusalem in 587. For most of the time his message was a denunciation of the people's sins and a forecast of disaster. The sins were much the same as those castigated by previous prophets, idolatry, profligacy and social oppression. Idolatry needs no references; the charge occurs in almost every chapter. For the rest see 2.34; 5.1–10, 23–35; 7.1–15; 9.4–6; 22.1–7; 23 (a denunciation of false prophets reminiscent of Micah). Unlike Isaiah, Jeremiah from the first forecast the fall of Jerusalem and the sack of the Temple. What is remarkable about Jeremiah is his intimate wrestlings with God. He speaks in the most frank and bold way with God, even claiming that God has deceived him; see for example 12.1–6; 20.7–12. Jeremiah does not enjoy his grim task of forecasting disaster and frequently protests against it. But he never forsakes his calling. Though he had no idea of life after death, he remained faithful to his prophetic task to the end. See the last passage we have referred to. There is some element of hope in his message. He utters the famous prophecy of the new covenant (see 31.31–37).

Among the smaller prophets Habakkuk stands out for his declaration of faith in 2.1–4. Appalled by the advances of the new conqueror from the north, Babylon, he yet declares the 'righteous shall live by his faith', a text of which Paul makes much use in Romans 1.17 and Galatians 3.11, and which we also meet in Hebrews 10.37–39.

In the anonymous prophet of the exile whose words are contained in Isaiah 40–55 we meet him who is probably the greatest of the prophets. The main burden of his message is one of liberation. God, he says, is raising up Cyrus the Persian conqueror in order to overthrow Babylon, permit Israel to return to their home country, and rebuild the Temple. In verses of moving poetry he announces the coming deliverance and depicts God as the only God in the universe, the master of history, and the saviour of Israel. See for example chapters 40; 43; 44.21–45.8; 45.18–25. Interspersed with all this is a contemptuous rejection of Babylonian idolatry; cf. 44.9–20; 46.1–4. But most important of all are the four 'Servant Songs': 42.1–4; 49.1–6; 50.4–11; and 52.13–53.12. In these passages the prophet describes one whom he calls the 'Servant of the Lord'. We learn that this servant is specially called and trained by God in order to speak God's word to Israel. He is to meet scorn, rejection, suffering, and apparently death. But by his obedient suffering he will bring about redemption. Moreover, there is even a hint that the Servant himself will be in some way rewarded after death. There is no certainty about the identity of the person whom the prophet had in mind when he composed these servant songs; but they have had a very great influence upon the writers of the New Testament, and, as we maintain, on Jesus himself.

Ezekiel is a strange figure; he is so many things at once: prophet, priest and even apocalyptist. He was carried away with the select group who were deported from Jerusalem to Babylon in 597 BC and all his prophecies are uttered from exile. Until the fall of Jerusalem in 587 BC he continuously denounces the sins of those left in Judaea, particularly idolatry. Once the city has fallen, he devoted himself rather to encouragement about the future. He ends with a blueprint for the rebuilding of the Temple (chs 40–48) which some scholars attribute to a later hand. Most bizarre of all is his initial vision of God narrated in ch. 1, so startling in describing God as presenting 'a likeness as it were of a human form' (1.26), that later Jewish tradition tended to try to put him on the Index of prohibited books.

Daniel is not a prophetic book at all, but a piece of underground literature written in time of persecution (167–165 BC) in order to encourage the faithful to stand firm. Jonah is not a prophetic book either, but a brilliant little parable, written after the return from exile as a protest against the exclusive and introverted religion of the returned exiles. Of the rest of the prophetic corpus, Joel seems to belong to a late period. It mentions the Greeks (3.6). It is chiefly valued for its picture of the pouring out of the Spirit in the end time (2.28–29). Zephaniah, Nahum, Obadiah and Haggai and Malachi, have little to offer in the way of vital prophecy. The third part of the book of Isaiah, chapters 56–66, consists of a collection of prophecies belonging to the period of the return from exile. It contains some fine, lyrical passages describing the future glory of Zion (chapters 60–62). Among these occurs the famous proclamation of the prophet's anointing with the Spirit, which Jesus took up in the synagogue at Nazareth (see Isa. 61 and Luke 4.16–30). Though there is much of interest in these chapters, none of them reached the sublime level of insight attained by the author of chapters 40–55.

This leaves us with the Book of Zechariah, a strange and enigmatic work for the most part. The first eight chapters date from the year 422–416 BC during which time the rebuilding of the Temple was undertaken. The author of these passages, the true Zechariah, seems to be under the impression that Zerubbabel, the Jewish governor appointed by the Persians, was the Messiah, or at least God's destined prince. See Zechariah 4.1–10; 6.9–14. In this latter passage it is held by many scholars that the name of Joshua the high priest has been substituted for that of Zerubbabel after it has become clear that Zerubbabel was not going to enact the rôle of Messiah. Chapters 8–14 of Zechariah come from a later period, though there is no agreement among scholars as to when exactly they should be fitted in. Some put them as late as the Greek period (after 333 BC). They are full of strange events and enigmatic references. It is becoming clear that they have greatly influenced the gospel narratives, especially perhaps the Fourth Gospel.

It will be noticed that there has been very little reference to messianic prophecy in this survey of the canonical prophets. In fact we have passed over some passages that have traditionally been regarded as messianic prophecy. For example in Micah 5.2–4 there is a prophecy that a ruler will come forth from Bethlehem in Judah who will feed God's flock 'in the majesty of the name of the Lord his God'. Though this passage probably comes from a time later than Micah's, it certainly does forecast the restoration of Israel under a ruler of the lineage of David. Similarly in Jeremiah 23.5–6 the prophet envisages a time when there will arise a righteous king from David's line. In his days Israel will be saved and he will be called 'The Lord our righteousness'. It is difficult not to see here a criticism of the last king of Judah; his name was 'Zedekiah' which means 'The Lord is righteous'. But Zedekiah was very far from living up to his name.

Jeremiah hints that the king who is to come will really exhibit Jahweh's righteousness in his life.

Why have we not paid more attention to these passages? Because, even if they are 'messianic' prophecies in the strict sense of the term, they do not tell us very much about God. They tell us that already by about 600 BC the Jews, or some among the Jews, believed that at the end time there would be a righteous king of the lineage of David who would rule Israel justly. We cannot say that either author of these two passages consciously foresaw the coming of Jesus of Nazareth. Indeed, it might well be seriously suggested that Jesus of Nazareth was not the Messiah in the strict sense of the term. This is not to claim that somebody else has been, or ever will be, the Messiah instead of Jesus. But the 'messianic' element as such accounts for relatively little in the actual career and work of Jesus. Certainly the early Christians from the time of the resurrection onward regarded him as having fulfilled the rôle of the Messiah; hence his name 'Jesus Christ', Jesus the Anointed One. But Jesus himself showed no great enthusiasm for the title. His own understanding of messiahship was so different from the widely held one that the two had very little in common. He believed indeed that the new age promised from so long ago was about to dawn. He preached the imminent arrival of God's kingdom. His own ministry and death were, he believed, intimately connected with that event. But he did not go about claiming to be Messiah. His messiahship was esoteric in the sense that only those who understood the necessity of his death could know in what sense he was Messiah. The element of kingship, power and rule which formed the very essence of a widely held idea of the Messiah was absent from his vocation. It seems likely that the strong emphasis on the kingship of Jesus which we meet in the Fourth Gospel is a contribution to the christology made by the author of that gospel (indeed the same could be said of the First Gospel). Jesus' relation to the Old Testament has very little to do with messiahship, though, as we shall be seeing, it has a great deal to do with God. In as far as the Messiah was thought of as inaugurating the new age, the 'world to come', the kingdom of God, it was important that Jesus should be regarded as Messiah. The writers of the New Testament are convinced that with the ministry, death and resurrection of Jesus the new age, the messianic era, has dawned. But when we have said this we have said almost all that connects Jesus with the *rôle* of Messiah. His fulfilment of Old Testament prophecy transcended the category of messiahship. Messianic prophecy as such in the Old Testament is therefore of relatively minor significance.

IV

Nearly all the prophets whose work we have been considering had one element in common: they looked forward to a time when God would fully manifest himself, sin would be overcome, and the righteous, or perhaps we might rather say the faithful in Israel, would be vindicated. During the period we have been reviewing it was generally taken for granted that this vindication would take place in history, though in Ezekiel and in the Second Zechariah (chapters 8–14) there are hints of an 'apocalyptic' conclusion, i.e. that the vindication would mean the end of history as we know it, the end of this age and the beginning of a new age. Between the time of the latest canonical prophets and the birth of Jesus this apocalyptic expectation was greatly enhanced. We can see this reflected in the Book of Daniel, which is by far the latest of the books of the Old Testament to be written. There may be one exception to this forward-looking element in the prophets, the very earliest of them all, Amos. If we do not include the more hopeful verses at the end of his prophecy, which are probably not from Amos himself, there is no sign of a vindication in Amos. We simply do not know whether, if he had uttered God's word for the southern kingdom, he would have included this element. In fact he confined himself to speaking God's word to the northern kingdom. For them apparently he saw no hope. It must be confessed that history proved him right as far as the northern kingdom was concerned.

In all the other prophets, however, we do find this element of looking forward. In Isaiah it takes the form of a description of the Golden Age to come. In Jeremiah the future age will bring a new covenant, according to which Israel will obey God intuitively. In the anonymous prophet of the exile the Golden Age is about to dawn in which Israel will march home straight across the desert by an elevated road specially made for them by God, with water and shade miraculously provided. See Isaiah 40.3–4; 41.17–20; 42.16; 43.19–21; 49.8–13; 51.9–11. Ezekiel looks forward to the rebuilding of Israel (e.g. 37.1–14), not to mention the picture of the restored Temple which is included in his prophecy. There are several passages describing the ideal future for Israel in the third part of the Book of Isaiah. See for example Isaiah 60–62.

Now we can legitimately claim that this forward-looking element in the Hebrew prophets was fulfilled in the coming of Jesus Christ. Jesus' own message was that 'the time is fulfilled, the kingdom of God has drawn near' (Mark 1.15). Jesus himself believed that with his ministry, and probably by means of his death and subsequent vindication by God the end time foretold by the prophets had actually dawned. Professor R. G. Fuller's phrase 'inaugurated eschatology' is probably the most accurate definition we can hope for to describe Jesus' attitude to the future. Through his teaching runs this strong vein of fulfilment (cf. Matt. 13.17; Luke 10.24; and also Luke 4.21–27). What was fulfilled was the prophetic expectation of the time when God would fully reveal himself.

When we turn to the earliest records of the Christian church, i.e. the letters of Paul, we find this sense of prophetic fulfilment just as much in evidence. Compare I Corinthians 10.11, where Christians are described as those 'upon whom the ends of the ages have come'. Indeed Paul could not have written as boldly as he did about the significance of the sufferings of himself and his fellow-workers if he had not believed that they were living in the new age. See for example I Corinthians 4.10–13. The same belief in the advent of the new age runs through the early speeches in Acts 2.16–36; 3.18–26; 13.26–33. This belief is also implicit in the Fourth Gospel. John's references to the coming era of the Spirit carry this implication; see 7.39; 14.16, 26. We can also find references to the new age in Hebrews; see Hebrews 6.5, where believers can already prove for themselves 'the powers of the age to come'.

In this sense therefore the prophetic message was fulfilled in the coming of Jesus. The future to which they had looked had come to pass and God has revealed himself fully. But this is a rather vague form of prophetic fulfilment. We can be more specific than this. As the prophets declared God's will and intentions for their contemporary situation they revealed something of God's nature and character. Because they had insight into the sort of person God is, they were able to convey a picture of the ways of God. This was partial and fragmentary, as we shall be seeing; but a picture of who God is was gradually formed. We can look at each of the prophets we have mentioned and ask ourselves how much of God's character was revealed by the message which each prophet uttered.

Amos' great contribution to our knowledge of God lay in his emphasis on God's righteousness. God desires social justice, fair dealing. Worship and festivals held in honour of God divorced from any sense of obligation to live according to God's standard of righteousness are worse than useless. To us today this seems elementary, but not to the Israelites of the northern kingdom in Amos' day. Many of them apparently believed that God could not possibly complain as long as he received the statutory sacrifices and the appointed feasts were duly observed, as they certainly were. Against this complacent belief Amos' emphasis on God's requirement of righteous conduct and social justice was of the utmost significance for the future.

Hosea, as we have seen, also condemned the contemporary neglect of social justice. But he had something else to say about God. God loves Israel. So deeply does he love her that even her rebellion and apostasy will not induce him to abandon her. It may be worth while looking again at that eleventh chapter of Hosea which we have already noticed. In this chapter Hosea represents God as being the subject of conflicting emotions: his indignation at Israel's infidelity is urging him to abandon her altogether, but his love will not allow him to do this. His love must prevail, and Israel, though disciplined, will not be deserted. Here then we have an all-important insight into God's nature: he loves those whom he has chosen. This is not yet a universal love, but it is a love which was to have profound echoes in the New Testament.

Isaiah and Micah both reinforce the message that God demands social justice. And Isaiah couples with his declaration of God's righteousness a strong emphasis on his holiness. He will not endure evil; sinners must feel appalled in his presence.

We cannot say that Jeremiah has any new revelation to offer about God's character, but we can certainly claim that he shows an intimacy and boldness in God's presence unexampled among the prophets. As we have seen he actually accuses God of having deceived him (20.7). God had promised him protection (see 18.18–19), but his ministry had brought him nothing but hostility and danger. I think we can also suggest that the example of Jeremiah's life did provide new insight about God's relation to his faithful servants. There is no indication anywhere in Jeremiah's works that he believed in life after death, and his task of uttering God's message brought him a lifetime of suffering and hostility. But so strong was his sense of vocation that he never relinquished his mission. We may learn from Jeremiah that those who serve God must expect suffering.

It is difficult to discover any new or deeper insight into God's character in the prophecies of Ezekiel. It is true that he declares with absolute conviction and no little repetition that God does not punish the son for the sins of the father, a belief that runs quite contrary to the view held in earlier times. See Ezekiel's chapter 18. But this truth had already been understood by Jeremiah: see Jeremiah 31.29–30. And we also find it in Deuteronomy 24.16. Perhaps we may claim that Ezekiel gave it maximum publicity.

When we reach the anonymous prophet of the exile whose works are found in Isaiah chapters 40–55, we have reached the highest point of prophetic insight in the entire Bible. In the first place this is the first prophet to announce with absolute clarity that Jahweh is the only God; see 40.12–26; 42.5–9; 43.8–13; 45.1–7, 18–25; 46.8–11; 54.4–5. He is both sole God and sole creator, and he is the Lord of history, who has taken Cyrus by the hand in order that he may release Israel from exile. This notion of monotheism seems perfectly obvious to us today. Among us anyone who believes in God believes in one God. We do not meet genuine polytheism in the West. Even the atheist denies the existence of the God of Paul, of Augustine and of Thomas Aquinas, not the gods of ancient paganism. But in the sixth century BC in the middle east this was by no means obvious. Israel had to achieve an understanding of God as one, before in the time of the church men could begin to understand him as Three in One. It is the anonymous prophet of the exile who puts the coping stone on Israel's monotheism.

Next, this prophet portrays God as a saviour as no other Old Testament prophet does. God, he says, is about to achieve an act of salvation comparable to that which he accomplished when he made the world, or brought Israel up out of Egypt. See 41.8–10, 17–20; 42.10–17; 43.1–7; 44.6–8; 45.22–25; 51.9–11; 52.7–12. Of course previous prophets declared that God would save his people from adversity. We think especially of Isaiah of Jerusalem who confidently assured king Hezekiah that God would save Jerusalem from the Assyrian menace. But the anonymous prophet of the exile makes God's saving power a leading characteristic of his nature. His message is mainly concerned with this salvation. Because God was here so plainly set forth as saviour it was easier for Christians six hundred years later to proclaim Jesus Christ as saviour of the world.

This prophet has, however, a deeper message yet to convey about God's character. When we read the Servant Songs to which we have referred above we begin to realize something of how God brings about his greatest acts of salvation. As God used the self-sacrificing ministry of the 'servant of the Lord' to bring about Israel's redemption from the tyranny of sin, so he always uses the obedience of his faithful servants to bring about his most lasting results. Though we cannot be sure who the prophet had in mind when he wrote this description of the servant of the Lord, this figure of the servant was to have very great influence on Jesus himself and on the writers of the New Testament. The vocation of suffering and death which the servant is represented as carrying out must have influenced Jesus. This is not to say that Jesus studied the servant songs as such. He knew nothing of a 'Second Isaiah'. But when we consider the unanimous witness of the evangelists that Jesus believed in the necessity of his suffering and death, it is hard to resist the conclusion that Jesus saw himself as in some sense fulfilling the destiny of the servant of the Lord, the righteous sufferer whose death would redeem Israel and whose vindication after death was included in God's promise. Jesus did not confine himself to reading the servant songs, or even Isaiah 40–55. There is much to be found about the destiny of the suffering servant in other parts of the Old Testament, notably in such Psalms as 22, 69 and 109. But because this great prophet of the exile attained the understanding that God brings about his purpose by means of the suffering and even death of his faithful servants, we can rightly claim that he reflects more of God's character than any other prophet in the Old Testament.

Perhaps we can see now in what sense the canonical prophets can be said to have prepared the way for the coming of Jesus Christ. By their determination to declare God's will for their generation they succeed, in a fragmentary and piecemeal manner, in giving a picture of God. He is the only God, a living God, creator and redeemer. He has pledged himself to care for Israel whom he loves, but this does not mean that he will condone her sins or exempt her from the consequences of her wrong-doing. He loves Israel and is always ready to forgive those in Israel who truly repent. Most astonishing of all, suffering and death undertaken in his service have redeeming value. Because the prophets had provided in their various ways such a picture of God, it is not surprising that when Jesus Christ comes, who has brought us the full revelation of God's character, he should be seen to have fulfilled their words. Since they were given a partial insight into God's character, when the full picture of who God is is presented to us in Jesus Christ, it is only natural that we should see the correspondence between what Jesus was and what the prophets said about God. It is not a question of a miraculous endorsement of predictive vision. It is rather that the prophets give us a preliminary sketch of God's character. Jesus presents us with the full, living picture. Of course there is a vital connection between the two.

Once we have understood in what way we should interpret the
fulfilment of Old Testament prophecy in the New Testament, it is
possible to turn back to some of the New Testament passages in which
Old Testament prophecies are quoted as having been fulfilled and to
see in them a genuine theological correspondence. We will take as our
examples two passages from Paul, both of which we have already
cited. The first is Romans 10.14–21. Here Paul begins by quoting two
passages from Isaiah 40–55, they are 52.7 and 53.1. The first
proclaims the good news of God's salvation. In the time of the
anonymous prophet of the exile the good news consisted in the
declaration that God was about to release Israel from exile. In the time
of St Paul the good news was that God had redeemed mankind
through Jesus Christ. The two correspond closely because the same
saviour God is the author of both series of events. The second
quotation emphasizes the strangeness of the deliverance, so that most
of Israel did not believe it. The same sequence was reproduced in
Paul's own day, when most of Israel refused to believe that God had
sent his Messiah and ushered in the new age of deliverance. We may
be sure that Paul, reading through chapters 52 and 53, which were not
separated into two chapters in his day, identified Jesus with the
suffering servant so mysteriously described in the rest of chapter 53.
Here then is genuine correspondence. Paul's quotation of the
anonymous prophet of the exile makes good sense to us today. We
could follow this up by noticing that other quotation from Isaiah
which Paul makes in this passage. In Rom. 10.20–21 he quotes Isaiah
65.1–2. This we would regard as coming from the third section of the
Book of Isaiah, a collection of prophecies dating from the time of the
return from exile. Paul quotes them in order to show that Israel's
blindness and obduracy has been prophesied. In its original context
Isaiah 65.1–2 must have referred to the Jewish community to whom
the prophet had been speaking. God was anxious to address them but
they would not listen. He wearies himself with appealing to a people
who have no ears for his message. Paul regards 65.1 as a prophecy of
the accession of the Gentiles. Those who originally had not sought
God because he had not originally made himself known to them are
now receiving the revelation (in Paul's view because God's own people
the Jews have largely rejected it). We might even suggest that in the
picture of God holding out his hands in appeal there is a hint of the
cross. Though the correspondence is not as close as in the quotation in
Rom. 10.15–16, we can surely see that there is a genuine connection
here.

The other passage which we have already mentioned is Romans 15.3 and 9. Here Paul begins by quoting Psalm 69.9. He believes that these words are a prophetic utterance by the pre-existent Christ, foretelling his sufferings which he claims were inflicted on him because he was God's representative. We cannot of course interpret this verse from the Psalms in exactly this sense. If we are asked what the verse originally meant we must reply that it is the psalmist speaking to God: he declares that he suffers insults because he stands up for God's cause. His zeal for God has brought this contumely upon him. But it is not at all difficult to apply this to Jesus: he was insulted, tortured, and put to death because he was what he was, God's last word to Israel, the Son of God, God's representative come to bring in the kingdom of God. What was exemplified on a smaller scale in the case of the psalmist (whatever his date and circumstances) was shown forth on a cosmic scale by the fate of Jesus Christ. All God's faithful servants are vindicated in the sufferings, death and resurrection of Jesus Christ.

The other quotation, that which occurs in Rom. 15.9, is not so straightforward. Paul takes a verse from Psalm 18.49 (also found in II Sam. 22.50) and interprets it as an utterance of Jesus Christ to the Father. He prophesies the entrance of the Gentiles into the company of God's people and foresees Christ as praising God in the worship of the mixed Jewish-Gentile church of Paul's day. Can we make any sense of this? The original psalm is a thanksgiving to God (perhaps composed by David) because God has given victory over enemies. Verse 49 does not imply that the nations, i.e. non-Jews, will acknowledge the true God. The author of the psalm only asserts that the nations will be impressed by the power of David's God. We cannot accept Paul's assumption that the pre-existent Christ is speaking in this psalm, but we can perhaps see something in the notion of thanking God among the Gentiles. Paul thinks of the risen Christ as praising God in the worship of the church. The theology of a slightly later period would probably have said that Christians worship God through Christ in the Holy Spirit. Paul had not yet worked out clearly the relation of the risen Christ to the Holy Spirit. We might therefore put it like this: David praises God in the presence of both his own people and the surrounding non-Jews, many of whom he had conquered. The Christian church in the power of the Holy Spirit praises God for what he has done in Christ, that church being composed of Jews and Gentiles alike.

We have had to go a long way round in order to make any sense today of Paul's citation of Psalm 18.49 in Romans 15.9. Many other Old Testament citations in the New Testament would require an even more elaborate explanation in order to justify the claim that there was any real connection between the passage and the New Testament event. And in the case of many of them we would have to conclude that we can see no real connection at all. To take another example from those we have already referred to: in Matthew 2.15 it is claimed that the flight of the holy family to Egypt fulfils the prophecy in Hosea 11.1: 'out of Egypt have I called my son.' We have already observed that this verse in Hosea has a profound significance in itself, without any necessary reference to the New Testament: it harks back to God's gracious election and calling of Israel shown in the events of the exodus. If we are to make any sense of the interpretation claimed in Matthew 2.15 we must be prepared to regard Jesus Christ as being in his day the true representative of Israel. In himself he is obedient Israel, the only totally obedient Israelite. But even so, there is nothing particularly significant in his going down to Egypt and returning again as a child. Egypt was not for him the house of bondage. The author of the First Gospel seems here to be straining the sense of scripture. Hosea is one of the greatest of the Old Testament prophets, but we do not admire him because he foresaw the flight into Egypt. He did not foresee it in fact: he has a much deeper message to deliver than a miraculous prophecy of an event (if it was an event) that took place seven hundred and fifty years later.

If we want an example of an alleged fulfilment of prophecy in the New Testament that makes no sense at all to us today, we can surely find it in Hebrews 1.8–12. Here the author of Hebrews quotes Psalm 102.25–27 on the assumption that it is God the Father bearing witness to the eternity of God the Son. In fact when originally written it was a confession of the eternity of God on the part of the psalmist, in contrast to the ephemeral nature of his own existence. The psalmist when he wrote it had no notion of there being two divine entities. If the author of Hebrews chooses to treat it as an utterance of the Father to the Son, that is a purely arbitrary interpretation. It does not prove anything at all.

Before we finish, one other point needs to be made. We have claimed that the prophets witnessed to the nature and character of God by means of their respective messages, which were always addressed to their own time and circumstances. But this feature is not peculiar to the prophets. We can say indeed that many other parts of the Old Testament witness to God's character and nature: legend, history, the poetry of the Psalms, the stories in the Books of Ruth and of Daniel, all witness to the faith of the greatest minds in Israel. In as far as they rightly interpreted God's will in their day, they tell us about God. This is even true of a difficult work like the Book of Job. It is a 'protestant' book in the sense that its author is protesting against the generally accepted belief in his day that prosperity was a reward of piety and misfortune a punishment for sin. By his very protest he leads us into questions of theodicy and the problem of the suffering of the innocent. Though he has no clear solution on offer, he had led us into a better understanding of God. It is not surprising that there are definite links between the thought of the Book of Job and the theology of St Paul. But the prophets of the Old Testament, by their declaration that they speak in God's name and by their direct appeal to Israel's conscience, seem to have established a claim to more direct fulfilment in the New Testament. The greatest insights about God's nature are to be found in the prophets. Christianity when it first appeared must have had some of the characteristics of a 'back to the prophets' movement. It is in the prophets that we can most clearly and most easily trace the fulfilment of the Old Testament in the New.

Such then is our account of Old Testament prophecy and its connection with the New Testament. We have rejected the traditional view with its reliance on a theory of miraculous foresight. But we believe that we have shown how a genuine connection can be seen between the Old Testament prophets and the coming of Jesus Christ, so that he can join with sincerity in what the Nicene Creed says about the Holy Spirit: 'He spoke by the prophets.'

Chapter Eight

An Analysis of the Books of the Bible

In our exposition of prophecy we have dealt sufficiently with the prophetic books of the Old Testament, including the book of Daniel, which, as we have seen, is not really a prophetic book at all. We must now look at the other books of the Bible, trying to establish what sort of category each falls into and what light they throw on our knowledge of God. We begin with the Pentateuch, the first five books of the Old Testament, regarded as the centre of the Bible by Jews, because in them is enshrined the law of Moses. We must make a distinction first of all: the first four books, Genesis, Exodus, Leviticus and Numbers, are distinct from the fifth, Deuteronomy. Deuteronomy can be dated fairly accurately. It is usually connected with Josiah's reformation in 621 BC, narrated in II Kings 22–23. It has often been suggested that the book found in the Temple (II Kings 22.8) was actually the book of Deuteronomy, or an early version of it. At any rate Deuteronomy is a recasting of the Law, undertaken perhaps between 620 and 520 BC in the light of the teaching of the prophets. Its attribution to Moses is a literary convention.

The first four books, though they appear to give a connected narrative, consist in fact of at least three originally separate elements. These three elements run all through the four books. They have been blended together to form the books as we have them by an editor who lived well after the return from exile in Babylon. The three elements are usually dated thus: the earliest at about 800 BC, the second perhaps fifty or a hundred years later, and the third belonging to the period of the exile or later. But there is much dispute about the dates of these three elements or sources. Some scholars would put them all a good deal later. We have a good example of the blending of these sources in Genesis chapters 1 and 2. Genesis 1.1–2.3 comes from the latest of the three. It is an orderly, quasi-scientific account of creation, culminating in the creation of *homo sapiens*. Genesis 2.4–3.24 comes from the

earliest of the sources. It is a folk tale, full of uninhibited anthropomorphisms: God walks in the cool of the garden after the day's work
(3.8); he is afraid that mankind may attain immortality against God's
will (3.22). This alternation of sources can be traced all through the
first four books, though in Leviticus the latest source predominates,
and there is probably a fourth source as well.

As far as the material is concerned, we must class all the first eleven
chapters as story or myth or parable or saga (all these names have been
applied to them). They do not contain any scientific information
about the world or the origin of mankind. They represent the attempt
of Israelite writers to explain to themselves how the world and
mankind originated, on the basis of the traditional myths and stories
which have been told in Israel or learned from surrounding peoples
during the centuries. When we come to Abraham and the patriarchs,
we are still not yet in touch with history. The patriarchs are not
historical characters. They *may* represent tribes or parts of tribes.
With the appearance of Moses, the story of the exodus and the
wanderings in the wilderness, and the making of the covenant and the
law-giving on Sinai-Horeb, we are fairly and squarely in the realm of
legend. Legend is not fiction, but history seen through the mist of
distance. Certain events stand out: the deliverance from Egypt, the
creation of Israel as a people, the actual figure of Moses. But all *details*
are legendary.

The value of the Pentateuch to Christians is not that it gives us a
reliable account of how a divinely authorized law was given to Israel.
It lies rather in the picture of God which we find represented in it. It is
not a wholly consistent picture: the desert demon who demands
Gershon's foreskin in Exodus 4.24–26 is very different from the
majestic creator of Genesis 1. But we can see a picture of God
emerging over the centuries which it took to create the Pentateuch as
we have it. And often we can see how the strong belief in a personal
God can transform traditional myths, shared perhaps with other near
eastern peoples, into a vehicle for profound religious truth. This can
surely be said of the story of the garden of Eden, which for all its folk-
tale form presents a true picture of the relation of fallen man to a holy
God.

With the Books of Joshua and Judges we begin to encounter actual
history, though it is still very much wrapped up in legend. The editor
of Joshua writes on the later assumption that Israel conquered Canaan
in one campaign, but evidence to be found in other parts of the book
shows that it was a much slower process, and consisted partly of

assimilation with the Canaanite peoples. The Book of Judges is likewise built on a framework of apostasy and repentance corresponding to conquest by strangers and deliverance from their yoke. This framework is unhistorical, but there are distinct historical elements to be found in the book, not least, as we have seen, the Song of Deborah in chapter 5, which is a contemporary triumph song after the defeat of Israel's enemies.

The Book of Ruth belongs to the latest division of the Hebrew Bible and will be dealt with there. In I and II Samuel and II Kings we have the best efforts of Israel's historical writers to tell us the story of the people from the establishment of the kingdom with Saul and David until its fall and the Babylonian exile in 587 BC. As with the Pentateuch, so here we have a variety of sources to deal with. There is lively narrative, probably very close to contemporary history, in the 'Succession Narrative' which begins with the rise of Saul and brings us to the establishment of Solomon on the throne. But even here we have disparate elements. Notice the very different estimates of the kingship in I Samuel 9–11 compared with I Samuel 8 and 12; in the first passage the kingship is accepted as a good and necessary development approved by God; in the last two passages it is presented as a sinful movement on the part of Israel and really an encroachment on God's privilege. These last two, we may be sure, were written considerably later, when disillusion about the kingship was common. The Books of Kings give us something like an historical account of the kingdom, though there is still much legendary material, such as the stories about Elijah and Elisha. The first editor made a valiant effort to calibrate the regnal years of the kings of the northern and of the southern kingdom respectively; but he is not entirely successful. The regnal years of the kings of each kingdom do not tally as they should.

The two Books of Chronicles, and the Books of Ezra and Nehemiah come from a period well after the return from exile; Chronicles probably can be dated about 350 BC. It is a representation of Israel's history, looked at nearly half a millennium after many of the events, from a very sacerdotal point of view. David is idealized; the kings of Judah are represented as far more powerful than they actually were. It does not give us very much more historical information. The Book of Ezra is likewise a document of dubious historical value. It is not clear when Ezra lived, if indeed he lived at all. Nehemiah on the other hand is a three-dimensional historical figure. We seem to have his actual account of his mission to Judah, some time in the fifth century BC.

What do these historical and quasi-historical books mean to us

Christians? We cannot help being interested in the story of Israel, since our religion sprang out of Israel's religion. Every now and then we are greatly struck by an insight into God's nature, as when Nathan condemns David for abducting the wife of Uriah the Hittite and having Uriah killed (II Sam. 12.1–15). We admire Micaiah's courage in pronouncing God's judgment on Ahab in I Kings 22; and we are impressed by Nehemiah's faith and integrity as governor of Judaea under the Persian Empire in rebuilding the walls of Jerusalem in the face of great difficulties. We are under no obligation either to approve of Saul's slaughter of the Amalekites (I Sam. 15), nor of Elijah's slaughter of the prophets of Baal (I Kings 18), nor of Jehu's slaughter of the house of Ahab (II Kings 9.21–10.11). Hosea himself condemns this last: see Hosea 1.4.

In the third part of the Hebrew scriptures the Book of Psalms holds pride of place. It was the hymn book of the Jewish people and of the Temple while it stood. It contains psalms which originated in all periods of Israel's history. The traditional view that David wrote all the Psalms is mistaken; one or two (e.g. Psalms 18, 24) may date from his time. Others are plainly from the time of the exile (e.g. Psalm 137), or come from the period when the Torah had become the centre of Israel's religion (e.g. Psalm 119). In themselves they constitute a rich treasury of devotion. Here we find the most heartfelt expressions of faith in a personal God (cf. Ps. 42, 43, 63). No wonder that the Christian church has been able to use them in its daily worship from the earliest times. The Book of Proverbs is a collection of proverbs; some may go back to Solomon, but most come from a later period. The most significant part of the book from the point of view of Christian theology is Proverbs 8.22–end, the great poem on Wisdom. It probably dates from the third century BC when Israel was under Greek rule and was experiencing the impact of Greek education and culture. The Book of Daniel, which also belongs to the third division of the Hebrew Bible, has already been referred to (see pp. 73, 78 above). The Book of Job stands alone in the Bible. Written some time after the exile, it is a brilliant poem, an exposé of the current orthodoxy that only sinners suffer; the righteous must prosper. Job challenges this view and calls on God to do him justice. The denouement in chapters 38–42 is unexpected and impressive, but leaves all the questions unanswered. An answer is given to them in the New Testament. Ecclesiastes is written by someone who has tried to make sense of life and failed. He believes firmly in God and God's providence, but can see no purpose in human existence. It was written during the period of

Greek rule. This division of the Hebrew Bible also contains two *novelle*, short stories enshrining a moral. The moral is much the same in each. In both the Book of Ruth and the Book of Jonah it is suggested that God is interested in non-Jews, contrary to contemporary Jewish exclusivism. Neither book should be treated as history, but both are magnificent examples of 'a story with a moral'. Esther might fall into this category, except that the moral is much less important. Perhaps originally written to explain the origin of the feast of Purim, it is a book that seems to have nothing to say to Christians. The same could be said of the Song of Solomon. Originally written as a lovesong, or a set of lovesongs, it has been treated allegorically by both Jews and Christians. But there is no sign in the book itself that it is intended to be understood as an allegory. It should be added that none of the books attributed to Solomon was written by him, neither Proverbs, nor Ecclesiastes, nor the Song of Solomon, nor the book of Wisdom in the Apocrypha. Just as it was traditional to assign law-books to Moses and psalms to David, so it was traditional to assign wisdom books to Solomon. We shall find traces of the same practice in the New Testament.

We have discussed the prophets in chapter seven. When we turn to the New Testament we find that we are dealing with very different material. The New Testament has a unity of theme that is much less obvious in the Old Testament. All the books of the New Testament were written in order to witness to Jesus Christ and to encourage Christians in the faith of Christ. Of the four gospels the first three (usually called synoptic) have clear connections with each other. The Fourth Gospel stands apart. It is on the first three gospels that we rely for all that we know about the historical Jesus, though they are not written as what we today would call biographies. They are written by Christians who believe in the resurrection of Jesus, and sometimes, especially in Matthew, we seem to be face to face with the risen Christ rather than the Jesus of history. But they are priceless sources of information about his life and teaching. The Fourth Gospel was written primarily in order to present a picture of Jesus as the Word incarnate. The author takes great liberties with historical facts, and does not hesitate on occasion to add to and even invent new teachings of Jesus. It might be said that his Jesus is always the risen Lord rather than the Galilaean prophet. No doubt there is historical fact to be found in the Fourth Gospel, but finding it is no easy matter.

Traditionally fourteen letters are attributed to Paul in the New Testament. From these we may abstract Hebrews at once. It does not claim to be written by Paul, and the early church knew perfectly well that Paul did not write it. It is a penetrating exposition of the meaning of the death of Christ, using the language of the Old Testament cult, but baptizing it into the service of Christianity. The thirteen letters attributed to Paul may be divided into three categories: those certainly written by Paul; those about whose Pauline authority there is serious doubt; and those that are in all probability not Paul's at all. Into the first class come Romans, I and II Corinthians, Galatians, Philippians, I Thessalonians, and Philemon; into the second category we put Colossians and II Thessalonians; into the third Ephesians, I and II Timothy and Titus. The genuine Paulines give us a wonderful insight into the life of the churches founded by Paul and of Paul's understanding of the significance of Jesus. Colossians, if not by Paul, was written by a close disciple who wished to apply the Pauline gospel to the condition of the church after Paul's death. Ephesians and the Pastorals (I and II Timothy and Titus) give us a picture of the Pauline churches in the generation after Paul. We should not be scandalized that those who regarded themselves as Paul's disciples used his name for their works. It was a recognized convention at the time, and indicated that they wished their writings to be regarded as belonging to the school of Paul.

Acts is the only history of the first thirty years of the church which we possess and is therefore of inestimable value. It was probably written in the nineties of the first Christian century. The very earliest years of the church's existence were already to some extent shrouded in legend, and this is reflected in Acts. But as we begin to follow Paul's career we find ourselves in contact with a real history. James is a strange document. It comes from an environment of a strongly Jewish Christianity, but is written in an excellent style of Hellenistic Greek. It may belong to the end of the first century. I Peter is a beautiful exposition of what early Christianity meant, full of Christian joy and enthusiasm. It seems to belong to a period when Christians were beginning to feel the opposition of the Roman government and must therefore be put early in the second century. It can hardly have been written by the apostle Peter. II Peter is certainly not by Peter. It was written perhaps as late as AD 120 and the writer based his work on the Epistle of Jude, perhaps a contemporary work. Both these 'letters' are late, among the latest in the New Testament. They are written to warn Christians against a form of false teaching that was prevalent. The three letters of John belong to the same school as the Fourth Gospel. Scholarly opinion seems to be coming to the conclusion that they are not by the author of the Fourth Gospel, but by a disciple of his.

The last book in the New Testament is *sui generis*, a Christian apocalypse. Written in the lurid light generated by the beginning of persecution on the part of the imperial authorities, it depicts in a series of startling scenes the war between the beast (the Devil who is the moving force behind the persecuting emperors) and the Lamb, the suffering church inspired by the crucified and risen Christ. The message is conveyed by means of expressive imagery nearly all taken from the Old Testament. In times of persecution the Book of Revelation comes alive; it has proved itself a perennial source of comfort and inspiration to the suffering church.

We have not space to deal adequately with the apocrypha, those books which appear in the Septuagint but not in the Hebrew Bible. They are recognized as fully part of the Old Testament by the Roman Catholic Church. On the whole they were written 'between the Testaments', though there is some overlap. They contain some material of great value for an understanding of the background to the New Testament, notably Ecclesiasticus or the Wisdom of Ben Sira, written about 180 BC by a Jew who had had wide experience of the world of diplomacy and affairs. The Wisdom of Solomon is an early attempt to come to terms with the wisdom of the Greeks without abandoning the religion of Israel; and if we did not have I Maccabees we would know very little about the Maccabaean freedom fight that finally delivered Israel from the yoke of Greek rule.

Chapter Nine

The Proportion of Faith

I

While we maintain that the right category in which to see the Bible is that of evidence, we do not want to give the impression that the Bible is simply a collection of ancient documents, the total evidence available for discussing a matter of ancient history, a number of miscellaneous documents bound together by a single subject, or combined in a single volume more or less casually. The form which the record of revelation takes is indeed that of a collection of ancient histories, letters, poems and so on. But all these ancient documents, Jewish and Christian, were written from faith to faith for a worshipping community by a worshipping community, by believers for believers. In the case of the Old Testament they have largely been shaped and modified by centuries of use in worship (the Psalter is an obvious example). Some of the documents may have been used expressly for use in worship (it has been suggested that this applies to I Peter, for example). Certainly from an early period they were read at worship, and were preserved, copied, circulated and studied because they fed, sustained, stimulated, awoke and refreshed faith. Read out of the context of a worshipping community, they become meaningless, incoherent and bizarre; the whole Old and New Testaments fall apart. In short, they are meant for use within a living tradition, which is still living today, and without that tradition they are liable to be misunderstood. This is not to say, as some people who ought to know better appear to be anxious to say, that the Christian or the church can read into them any nonsense at all because they are ours. We must be restrained by the demands of common sense and critical scholarship. But still, the Bible is not just literature. About fifty years ago some people, including George Bernard Shaw, produced a volume called *The Bible to be Read as Literature*. This production was about as sensible as producing an edition of *Hamlet* and calling it a 'Manual for Grave-diggers' or 'A Short Guide to Correct Acting', or as James Thurber once most amusingly narrated, it was like the woman who read through *Macbeth* assuming that it was a detective-story.

More than this, however, can be said of the Bible. It has a power of transcending its expounders. St Augustine in the late fourth and early fifth century had been taught, when he became a Christian, that the Psalms were a kind of transcript of a tape-recording made by David of conversations between God and Christ, a miraculous oracle full of Christian doctrine. But as he read them he could not help realizing that they were in large part the record of the existential encounter of individuals with God, and consequently absorbed this use of them into his own thought and his own prose. In the sixteenth century the thought of St Paul, as presented by the Reformers, broke up the mediaeval church's elaborate machinery for salvation and launched a new era in the history of Europe. In our own day a great return to the theology of the Bible has transformed the Roman Catholic Church and opened new possibilities of Christian reconciliation and reunion. This is because what the Bible records really were the acts of God, and the acts of a God who is not dead, but living and contemporary. Notice that we do not describe the Bible itself as the revelation of God. It is the human record of that revelation. This is the truth in the otherwise unsound and unsatisfactory idea that the Bible is a kind of extension of the incarnation, the 'inscripted' parallel to the incarnate Word. Origen first produced this idea (*Commentary on Matthew* XV.3), and it has since been occasionally taken up by some Protestants and by a very few Catholics. In fact, there is no genuine parallel between the perfection of human moral character which we see in the incarnation and the inerrancy of written propositions which some people have seen in the Bible, between the particularity of human life and the particularity of the written word. In short, as the Bible records the activity of God, so it has a time-transcending capacity which lies, not in its literary form but in its subject, and this capacity is entirely compatible with the Bible's normal conditioning by time and circumstance.

But if we speak of the Bible as being written 'from faith to faith', we should go on to ask, faith in what objects and in what order? Do we first believe the Bible and then believe in Christ, wholly by-passing the church? Protestant theologians have tended to teach this. Or do we first accept the church as our reliable guide and then believe (with varying degrees of assent) what the church teaches, including, among other things, what the church says that the Bible teaches? This is traditional Roman Catholic teaching, and this was one of the great differences between the Catholic Modernists at the beginning of this century and the theologians of their communion who had at that time the ear of the authorities in their church.

Neither of these positions will bear careful scrutiny. To begin with, there are different kinds of faith according to what you believe in, and it is possible to believe the same thing from different motives. One person may believe that the Labour Party will win the next general election because he has carefully studied the political situation and has so reached this conclusion. Another man may believe the same thing because he has persuaded himself that the eleventh chapter of the Book of Daniel has predicted it. Faith that Golden Boy will win the Kentucky Grand National on Tuesday is very different from faith in the capacity of a university education to improve the mind. Faith in the wisdom of an old friend is different from faith in the stars as guiding our destinies. So faith in the church, faith in the Bible and faith in Christ (or more accurately, faith in God in Christ) are three quite different things. One is faith in an institution, another faith in a book, and the third faith in a divine Being.

We must therefore distinguish chronologically. The Christian first has faith in the church which wrote and commends the Bible. There is no conceivable way in which the Christian can come at the Bible without the intervention of the church. Next, the Christian has faith in the Bible as witnessing to God's activity in Christ. Finally, the Christian has faith in God-in-Christ. The first two acts of faith are no more than preliminaries to the third, for God ultimately guarantees the authenticity of the other two.

The old Anglican formula of 'the church to teach, the Bible to prove' is as good a rough-and-ready guide to this subject as any other. But we must here reject the hoary old idea, which still raises its ancient head from time to time, that the Catholic accepts the judgment of the church, whereas the Protestant believes in exercising his private judgment. If the Catholic really surrenders all his private judgment to the church, he can only do so by an act of private judgment, because he is a thinking and feeling individual subject and nothing on earth can prevent him being so. And every time he renews his submission to the church he makes a new act of private judgment. Then the Protestant, however stout may be his defiance of ecclesiastical decisions and priestcraft, is wholly dependent on the church for his being able to read the Bible and in the vast majority of cases is very anxious to learn what the church has to say about the Bible, and, if he is an Anglican, repeats a complex interpretation of the Bible made sixteen centuries ago whenever he attends a celebration of the eucharist. This distinction between the Catholic and Protestant is a matter of degree, not of kind, and is becoming less applicable every year.

But before we leave this subject we must meet two objections to treating the Bible primarily as evidence. One suggests that the documents contained in it are too far removed from our time for us to use them effectively; the cultural and chronological gap is too great. The Bible, in both Testaments, is full of ideas, assumptions, the ordinary cultural furniture of that day, which are utterly remote and alien from us. One example is the *herem*, the practice of ritually massacring a whole community in order to dedicate them to a particular deity, which is to be found warmly approved of in the case of the people of Jericho, and of the Amalekites and several others in the Old Testament. Even Origen in the third century AD found this too much to stomach, and hastened to allegorize these incidents out of history. Another example is the belief that the world is full of invisible daemons or devils bent upon doing human beings harm; this belief is universal in both Testaments and was accepted implicitly by the whole ancient world, even by highly educated intellectuals like Origen. It is indeed difficult to avoid the conclusion that Jesus himself accepted it. But we in the twentieth century cannot possibly believe this sort of thing; only staunch fundamentalists believe it. Another example is the belief that God speaks in thunder. In fact the whole pre-scientific view of the universe is part of the woof and warp of the Bible, including the unexamined assumption that sacrifice is the right way to approach God; this last was all pervasive in the religions of the ancient world and was only first challenged when Anselm wrote his *Cur Deus Homo* in 1098. One could produce several other instances. How can we hope to understand the thought of eras so far removed from us in time?

The other argument maintains that the documents of the Bible are too diverse or too scanty to support the weight of doctrine laid upon them. In what sense can we describe the Old Testament as a whole? Both Jews and Christians have used it for quite different purposes and in order to do so have employed illegitimate and futile exegetical techniques. Does not this suggest that the book is in fact unusable? The same argument can be applied to the New Testament. Criticism in this field now tends to be centrifugal rather than centripetal, to suggest that there is no central gospel or *kerygma*, only a series of diverse and perhaps contradictory interpretations. It tends to contrast rather than to harmonize the doctrine of Paul and of John, of the synoptics, of James, of the Revelation, and so on.

Again, the New Testament can be thought to give us no adequate basis upon which to build an acceptable doctrinal system. Our documentary knowledge of Jesus is confined to the New Testament. Other historical sources, Josephus, Tacitus, Suetonius and Pliny, are all late and their evidence tenuous. The evidence for the career and teaching of Jesus in the synoptics is not very large in bulk and is open to the charge that some of it has been altered during the period that it was orally transmitted. How far can we trust the historical veracity of John? There are only a very small number of facts about the life and message of Jesus added by the rest of the New Testament. It is contended that this is an inadequate foundation upon which to build the vast doctrinal structures which later tradition has erected upon them, or indeed to erect any doctrinal structure at all.

We certainly must not forget the avalanche of time that has fallen between us and the people of the Bible. It is inept to suggest that political or social situations which we find in it resemble at all situations in our own day, though this is a weakness to which many clergy are liable. But emphasis upon the cultural gulf which lies between us and the people of the Bible has been overdone. There can be and has been a continuity of culture between their day and ours. We owe a vast deal to the Greeks and the Romans who were, with the Hebrews, the founders of contemporary European culture. The idea, which has been mooted in some quarters, that cultures are wholes which cannot be fragmented and continued in part, but can only be transmitted in whole, is a peculiarly unconvincing one. There are almost no whole cultures, no cultures which have not been influenced by forces and ideas coming to them from outside. The nearest approach to such a thing is probably the culture of rural Northern Ireland, but even that cannot be called an inviolable whole. Cultures are always to some extent pluralist. And this was certainly true of the culture in which the ancient Jews found themselves (Egyptian, Phoenician, Babylonian, Canaanite), and just as true of the culture in which the New Testament was written and in which the Christian church began its career (Greek, Roman, Jewish, even Oriental). This plurality of culture was in fact a constant problem for the ancient church. We cannot therefore be cut off from the Bible by our inability to grasp its culture as a whole, because it was not a whole.

In fact as the Christian church in the first millennium of its existence continued to grow into every part of Europe and partly to influence and partly to absorb the culture of Europe, it managed to effect a remarkable fusion between some of the constituents of the dying pagan world with its own native Jewish culture. Quite apart from the question of how much paganism survived in a covert form, the Roman tradition of law and order and the Greek tradition of philosophical enquiry remained active and living within the culture of the Middle Ages. It has been suggested that the Greek tradition of free enquiry and appeal to reason combined with the Christian emphasis upon the importance and significance of the material world made the seed-bed for the rise of modern science. Cultures do not simply disappear. They can survive, or legacies from them can survive, for a very long time. Some people think that Ireland has not yet quite freed itself from the culture of the Neolithic period, as instanced by the Irishman's passionate love of funerals (cult of the dead surviving)!

If we wish to estimate how far we can understand or appreciate the ideas and behaviur of people of long past ages, we can make a useful comparison with ancient literature which is earlier than the first century AD and which had no connection at all with Hebrew culture. We can read Homer's two epics, the *Oresteia* of Aeschylus, the *Oedipus Tyrannus* and *Antigone* of Sophocles, Euripides' *Trojan Women* and *Bacchae*. We can read the works of Plato, of Aristotle, of Lucretius and of Vergil. Pre-Columbian art, the Great Wall of China, the carvings at Mahabalipuram in South India all came from cultures and civilizations widely different to ours. But they still appeal to us and evoke our admiration. It would be absurd to say that they do not touch us, that we cannot comprehend them, or that the effect which they make on us is something utterly different from that which they made on their contemporaries. On the contrary, at the Renaissance classical literature mostly underwent a revival and had a widespread effect upon the literature and art all through the fifteenth, sixteenth and seventeenth centuries. If these masterpieces from remote ages can speak to us poignantly in the twentieth century, we should not be afraid to allow that the Bible can also speak to us in its original terms.

This capacity to speak from a distant antiquity is particularly true of works of art. The monuments of the distant past are not merely dumb signs conveying no message, because we are ignorant of their original backgrounds. The cave-drawings in Lascaux, which go back thousands of years, Stonehenge, Carnac and Newgrange, which are the memorials of the Stone Age, can still cause wonder and delight in our breasts. The Parthenon, completed more than twenty-four centuries ago, can still be recognized as one of the supreme achievements of human genius. The Greek temples at Paestum in southern Italy remained little recognized for twelve and a half centuries until at the end of the eighteenth century they were rediscovered by English artists and architects and had a discernible influence on English art. One is almost tempted to say that great art is above time and transience and can speak to our souls, defying the battering siege of wrecking time. Of course, there are some ancient inscriptions and monuments which still baffle our attempts to understand their message, such as the Pictish sculptures and the designs on stones in Newgrange, and the Etruscan language. But to say that we are virtually cut off from the past and are indulging in an elaborate game of self-deceit when we try to decipher its remains is absurd, and is contradicted by the recent extraordinary increase in popular interest in archaeology, and by the growth in the number of museums in this country alone in recent years.

We can with caution use the appeal to a common humanity evident in the literature of the Bible. It is indeed a tasteless mistake to treat the stories of the patriarchs, those depositaries of ancient legend, myth and cultic practice, as if they were soap-operas comparable to 'Dallas' or 'Coronation Street'. And some of the stories in the Bible have ceased to appeal to us: the sin of Korah, Dathan and Abiram, the sin of stoning (with all his family) of Achan, the murder of Agag, the tale of Esther the king's chief concubine and the bloodthirsty massacre of Persians by Jews which rounds it off. But others retain their perennial freshness: the story of Ruth, the rebuking of David by Nathan the prophet, the story of David and Jonathan, the parables of the Good Samaritan and the Prodigal Son. Above all the figure of Jesus continues to appeal surprisingly. We might indeed ask whether he does not appeal to us more than he did to the men and women of, say, the early Middle Ages or the eighteenth century. We should note that the Bible has already survived several transplantations from one culture to another, and is continuing to do so in diverse parts of the world today. In some respects we understand it better than did the ancients. We can appreciate the Book of Job much more intelligently than could those who wrote commentaries on it in the first four or five centuries, all of whom failed to see its dramatic nature and the true inwardness of the subject which brings it before us. We are no longer troubled by the anthropomorphisms of the Old Testament as were the

Rabbis and the Fathers, and we can appreciate the story of Jonah as they apparently did not. We can admire the lofty poetry of Second Isaiah, placing him in his true context and century.

The question of the adequacy of the New Testament to bear the weight of doctrine put on it is not an easy one to answer in a small compass. It will be partly met when we come to speak about how to derive doctrine from the Bible. It is enough to say here that the words and deeds of Jesus are not the only evidence relevant to doctrine. Behind him lies the Old Testament and before him the Acts and Epistles, that is, the immediate reaction of the first Christians to his advent. Again, what counts is not quantity but quality. A single atomic bomb is more important than a million revolver shots. And finally, if God is to make a revelation of his nature, will and activity to the human race which shall be incapsulated in time and space, then perhaps he knows his own business best in causing it to have the form of a history and a human life and death rather than a philosophical thesis, a scientific discourse or declaration of general principles. Perhaps the story of Jesus Christ is in the end more resistant to the erosion of time than the pronouncements of Confucius or of Plato.

II

It shows scant respect for the Bible if one reads it without making any attempt to understand the circumstances in which it was written. Or, to be more exact, one should try to understand the circumstances in which each part of it was written. As we have seen, this does not mean merely asking in what historical order the books were written. It is frequently the case as far as the Old Testament is concerned that what comes before us as a single book is in fact composite: different parts of it were written at widely different times. Thus, we shall fail to understand the true meaning of Genesis 1–3 unless we realize that Genesis 2.4–3.24 is one of the earliest sections of the Old Testament, whereas Genesis 1.1–2.3 was probably written at least three hundred years later. If we read the two accounts as one continuous narrative it is as if we thought the plays of Shakespeare and of Bernard Shaw were all written by the same playwright. In a word, when studying any part of the Bible we must be prepared to try to find out, as far as it is ascertainable, when, why, by whom, and where that part was written.

One of the commonest forms of error is to ignore the fact that the Old Testament was written before the coming of Christ by people who knew nothing of Jesus of Nazareth. As we remarked in our section on the Fathers' interpretation of scripture, almost all the Fathers fall into this error. To take a very obvious example, St Augustine (*d.* AD 430) frequently quotes Psalm 85.11 as a prophecy of the incarnation. In his Latin version of the Psalms he had '*Veritas de terra orta est*', 'Truth has sprung out of the earth'; Jesus, argues Augustine, says, 'I am the truth', so this verse from the Psalms is a prophecy of his birth from a human mother. In fact the Hebrew word which is translated with '*veritas*' is better rendered 'faithfulness', as in the RSV of Psalm 85.11. The Psalm as a whole is an idealistic description of the golden age to come. As such, it is indeed appropriate to use it as the church does, at Christmas. But to describe Psalm 85.11 as a prophecy of the incarnation is going far beyond the evidence.

Similar examples of forgetting that the Old Testament is pre-Christian abound. How often, for instance has the story of Elisha and the bears in II Kings 2.23–24 been used by Christians as a way of teaching children respect for their elders! The small boys who mocked at Elisha were cursed by him and *therefore* forty-two of them were torn by bears! All the moral implications behind this are totally contrary to the gospel of Christ. To curse small boys because they are rude is not Christ-like; and to imagine that God would arrange so dreadful a punishment for so light an offence is opposed to everything which we learn about God from the New Testament.

This rule of observing the context holds equally when we read the New Testament. Paul, for instance, is frequently accused of not approving of marriage because in I Corinthians 7.8 he advised unmarried Christians not to contract marriage alliances. But those who so accuse him frequently fail to add that the reason for this advice was what he called 'the present (or impending) distress' (I Cor. 7.26) that is, his belief that the *parousia* was imminent. For the vast majority of Christians today therefore, since we have no reason to believe that the *parousia* was imminent, his advice on marriage is not relevant, far less obligatory.

In the same way, within the New Testament itself we must ask of any book, or any passage, 'who wrote it, and in what circumstances?' before we can fully benefit from what it has to say. Thus in I Timothy 2.12–15 we find what appears to be a very 'anti-feminist' view of women. They are not to dominate; they must not be allowed to teach; they are more gullible than men, because Eve was deceived by the serpent (whereas Adam apparently was not). They can be saved by child-bearing. Who wrote these words? Very probably not St Paul. It is much more likely that they were written by an admirer of Paul who borrowed his name as much as forty years after his death. For many educated Christians therefore this view of women does not carry the authority of the apostle of the Gentiles.

One final example may be adduced, perhaps, one with rather radical implications. What is the relevance of the Fourth Gospel to the Christian today? Most students who are acquainted with the background to this gospel would agree that it does not do what all Christians until a hundred and fifty years ago believed it did, that is, offer an authentic historical account of the words and deeds of Jesus of Nazareth. It follows that the relevance of St John's Gospel must lie in some other field. In fact of course it is an essential aid to the Christian understanding of Christ because in it are outlined the beginnings of that doctrine of the incarnation, and even of the Trinity, which the church eventually decided are essential for the full apprehension of Jesus Christ.

In a word, if you wish to avoid disastrous misunderstandings, you must attempt to study the Bible as a whole and in its parts in its context. 'What were the actual circumstances in which this book, or this part of this book, were written?' That is the question we must always ask. We cannot always find a fully satisfactory answer, but if we never even ask it, we shall never understand the Bible as we ought.

Chapter Ten

The Canon of Scripture

One could say without great exaggeration that the canon of the Old Testament has never been decided. The old canon was only gradually achieved. First, the Law (The *Torah*) was compiled and closed, some time after the return of the Jews from exile. Then, some considerable time after this, not finally perhaps until late in the second century BC, the prophetic canon was decided on, consisting of the three major prophets, Isaiah, Jeremiah and Ezekiel. Finally the Writings, the third division of the Old Testament, were grouped. But this is a schematic way of describing a much more untidy process. The canon of the *Torah* was closed early, but there were various documents and additions to the Prophets which were in an ambiguous relation to the canon by the first century BC at latest, such as the book of Baruch and additions to Daniel. And the exact limits of the Writings were not determined for the Jews till about AD 100. In fact from the second century BC onwards there was a quite indeterminate edge to the Old Testament. The Jews in Palestine recognized a stricter and shorter list of books, all of which had originally been written in either Hebrew or Aramaic. Greek-speaking Jews in Alexandria and elsewhere, however, used a considerably larger list of sacred books, some of which, such as Wisdom, had originally been written in Greek. With this went a number of imaginative tales designed to be enlargements of and embroidery upon the traditional stories of the Hebrew scriptures. The story of Susannah is one of these, the Book of Tobit another, and the bloodthirsty feminist tale of Judith and Holofernes. This type of literature was already known; the books of Ruth and of Esther are examples which found their way into the stricter canon. Ecclesiasticus is a book originally written in Hebrew early in the second century BC, but about 130 BC translated into Greek by the original author's grandson. It is in any language a noble piece of work. The Greek-speaking Jews of the Diaspora accepted and used it, but it was excluded from the Palestinian canon.

When the Christians came to take over the Old Testament and give it their own interpretation, they found the situation very fluid. And on the whole they were content to leave it so. Great concern for what books are canonical or inspired and what are not was not one of their preoccupations. As the early centuries went on some people and some councils made lists of canonical books, but this did not necessarily imply a rigid attitude to determining the old canon. In fact throughout the whole of the period of the ancient church and the period of the Middle Ages the books which were later called either 'apocryphal' or 'deutero-canonical' were regarded by the vast majority of Christians as on a level with the others. Jerome in the late fourth and early fifth century tried to distinguish between those which had originally been written in Hebrew, as the genuine canon, and the books which had (or which he thought had) originally been written in Greek, regarding the second lot as in some way inferior; he was a very good scholar, and took seriously the fact that there was a distinction between the two categories as far as authenticity went. But his efforts made very little difference. The East read its Old Testament in Greek anyway and simply refused to distinguish between the two categories. The West, though after about 400 it had an Old Testament which was mostly translated into Latin directly from the original languages, and not from a Greek version, continued to treat the 'apocrypha' on precisely the same basis as the other books.

At the Reformation the Reformed churches made a great display of rejecting the 'apocryphal' or 'deutero-canonical' books as inferior to the others. The churches stemming from the Reformed traditions of Calvin and from the radical reformers such as the Anabaptists, rejected the Apocrypha altogether. It is not normally read in public worship and members of these churches usually have no acquaintance with the Apocryphal books. The more liberal communions, such as the Church of England and some Lutheran churches, retained the books in the second category for reading in church, but made some official modification of them, saying that they were good for forming ethics and morals (in spite of Judith!) but must not be used for doctrine, or some such reservation. In fact it is greatly preferable to take the larger view of the ancient churches, the Roman Catholic and the Orthodox, and retain the 'apocrypha' on an equal basis with the books in the first category. As far as witnessing to the faith of the Jewish people and to their history too (e.g. in the books of Maccabees), they are as useful as the others, and to abandon them is to forfeit much fine material, such as the contribution of Wisdom and

Ecclesiasticus. It is only when one ventures upon the slippery ground of pronouncing some book 'inspired' and others not, that one runs into difficulties with the 'apocrypha'. The subject illustrates both how uncertain are the edges of the old canon (and therefore how impossible to apply the concept of inspiration effectively), and how necessary it is for us to regard the scriptures as evidence rather than as oracle.

The canon of the New Testament was established gradually, just as the old canon was, though over a shorter period, and a more unanimous decision was made about it. During the first four centuries at least there was considerable indefiniteness about what one might call the outer edges of the canon. By about AD 120 a collection of books comprising the synoptic gospels, Acts and most of the Pauline literature, Hebrews and Revelation had been widely used by Christian churches. Mid-second-century documents suggest that the Pastoral Epistles and St John's Gospel were not yet established as standard documents. It was perhaps only under the threat of Marcionism, which rejected the Old Testament altogether and made drastic reductions in the New, that by about 170 the concept of a New Testament canon was accepted and the Fourth Gospel and the Pastoral Epistles included in it. Over the next one hundred and fifty years the rest of the New Testament canon as we know it came to be accepted by the whole church. But it should be understood that by the time some of the latest written books were canonized, such as II Peter and II and III John, the church was too far removed from the primitive period for its historical judgment on the authorship or authenticity of such books to be worth anything. By the third century, however, the same assumptions about inspiration and inerrancy which had been made about the Old Testament were now being attached to the New. If we ask, what were the criteria which led the church to decide which books should be included, it is not easy to answer. Certainly the question of apostolic authorship cannot have been decisive, because if we list these works circulating together about 120 – Matthew, Mark, Luke, Acts, Romans, Revelation, Hebrews – there is only one apostolic author among them. Probably known antiquity was the clearest indication, and perhaps they were recognized as containing good doctrine according to all the tests of doctrine that the church could then apply.

Notice that this collection does not contain St John's Gospel, and notice that we do not include Hebrews or Revelation among those written by apostles. The Fourth Gospel was certainly written and in circulation by 120, but for a considerable time after its composition it was suspect by the mainline church and was quoted by Gnostic groups. It looked like a Gnostic gospel. We must remember that all the books of the New Testament had to compete against a large number of books claiming to be genuine acts and gospels and epistles and even apocalypses. It was only when some unmistakably orthodox and popular writers, Melito of Sardis and Irenaeus of Lugdunum (and especially the latter) championed the Johannine gospel, showed that it was not a Gnostic document and provided it with an unimpeachable (though in fact highly doubtful) historical pedigree, that it was accepted by the church at large. Even as late as 200 there were groups who refused to accept its authenticity and its doctrine.

The Epistle to the Hebrews was from the beginning a book whose authorship was entirely uncertain. It was known and appreciated early. I Clement (?120), *the Gospel of Truth* (?145), perhaps II Peter (?120) witness to it. But it experienced considerable difficulty in winning acceptance by the church as a whole, mainly because it could not be clearly seen as a letter of Paul. Apostolic authorship was by the second half of the second century a necessary passport for authenticity – or rather, what was thought to be or could plausibly be claimed to be apostolic authority. In this period apostolic origin was being also claimed for the ministry, the Rule of Faith and the creed. The Epistle to the Hebrews could not easily pass this test. Its use therefore underwent a slump. Clement of Alexandria (*c.* 200) and Origen (*fl.* 225–250) can only speculate about its authorship. Origen very honestly says that God alone knows who wrote it, but remarks that all the same it is full of good doctrine and he uses it freely. In the West from about 200 to about 370 it is wholly ignored, except for very patronizing recognition by Tertullian and its use by pseudo-Tertullian *Adversus Omnes Haereses* (by Pope Zephyrinus?). As late as Lucifer of Calaris' tirades against the Emperor Constantius II (360+) Hebrews is proscribed in the West. The East seems to have used it continuously, in spite of doubts about who wrote it.

The Revelation of St John had a precisely different fate. It was known a little before the middle of the second century, for Bishop Dionysius of Corinth quotes it in a letter. But it was regarded with suspicion by many writers in the Eastern church, by the very influential Eusebius of Caesarea, for instance, because of its millennial proclivities. Well-educated, rationally-minded churchmen did not then, any more than they do now, like to encourage unstable Christians to imagine that the eschatological rule of Christ on earth heralding the End might come any minute and that the world was going to end with conventional apocalyptic catastrophes very soon. They thought that Revelation was highly likely to encourage such wild fantasies. These writers were also quite sophisticated enough to realize that the style and content and approach of this book was so utterly different from those of St John's Gospel that they could not be by the same author. Dionysius of Alexandria in the middle of the third century says in a letter that he finds its style so un-Johannine that he cannot think that it is by St John, and its contents bizarre and mysterious, though he is not ready to discard it altogether. The West apparently suffered from no such doubts about it, but on the whole the writers of the West were markedly less educated and sophisticated than those of the East and less capable of exercising a critical judgment. Consequently it was not till the end of the fourth or even the fifth century that the whole church accepted this book into the canon.

What then is the significance of this authoritative list of sacred books? What exactly does it mean to draw a line between say, Ecclesiastes and Ecclesiasticus, or between the Lamentations of Jeremiah and the *Hodayoth* of the sect which produced the Dead Sea Scrolls, between II Peter and I Clement? Is the canon of the scriptures a kind of *cordon sanitaire* dividing 'inspired' books from uninspired books, books which (in the old Jewish phrase) 'defile the hands' from ordinary books which can be handled safely? Is there some quality discernible in all the biblical documents which is lacking in all other documents whatever? The answer must be clear enough from what has already been established: there is no uniform directly observable difference in quality between canonical and non-canonical books. Of course, some books of the Bible are of such a remarkable quality as to outsoar all other literature: Second Isaiah, Job, Amos and Hosea, the four gospels, Romans, Hebrews. But some are far from deserving this character: Judges, Esther, Leviticus, Chronicles, James, II Peter. And conversely some non-canonical books among the list of early Christian or late Jewish literature are of a markedly superior quality to some biblical literature: the *Hodayoth* to Ecclesiastes, the *Letters of Ignatius* to II Peter and Jude. The *cordon sanitaire* theory will not do.

What the scriptural canon provides is a collection of evidence, simply that and nothing more. The evidence must be sufficient; it need be neither perfect nor complete. It can contain irrelevant material and material of uneven quality. Evidence of this sort can be blurred at the edges as long as the central part sustains the main weight of the testimony. The canon is clear, firm and weighty in its main bulk, but it has ragged edges. It is like a light which is dazzlingly bright at the centre but whose brightness gradually reduces and shades off till we reach a twilight zone where it is hard to distinguish light from darkness. That is why it is unnecessary to labour in order to discover some unique quality in the biblical books which make them somehow inspired or sacred.

Why should the canon be closed? This question applies especially to the New Testament. Why should we not update the canon to include some of the works of the early Fathers, of Thomas Aquinas, of Dante, of Luther, of Shakespeare, of John Bunyan, of C. S. Lewis and Billy Graham? The answer to this query lies in the nature of the evidence of which the New Testament canon consists. It is early, as early and authentic as could be found. This does not apply to these other works, great or trivial. The New Testament is essentially historical witness to an event and to the immediate response of men and women to this event, the coming of Jesus Christ and the birth of the Christian church. It represents the record of revelation and response to revelation, of Christ-and-the-church. What makes the new canon distinct from other collections of Christian documents is its early attestation, the antiquity of its origin *as a collection*. Here it is unique. No other collection of documents could possibly rival it. It stands immovably between us and the foundation events of Christianity. Of course, we could subtract a few documents from it here and there and add a few uncanonical ones. But this could be done with only a few, and it would not affect the *skopos*, the burden, the effect of the whole. It would be a very upsetting and remarkably futile exercise. At a point in history when they were in a good position to judge, early Christians chose this new canon. We have no authority to add or subtract because we cannot go back to AD 70 or 100 or 120, and there are no strong reasons why we should attempt to do so.

Finally, we may ask, 'Is the Bible a whole?' This question has cropped up in another form already. We have observed that the Jews use the Old Testament for noticeably different purposes from those for which it is used by Christians. The Christians find little use for the Law, but the Jews prize this above all the rest. How can we regard the Old Testament as a whole, as a genuine base for doctrine, in these circumstances? Similarly the New Testament can be challenged. Does it seriously present a whole system or consistent scheme of doctrine or theology? It is difficult enough to say with conviction and integrity, 'The New Testament says . . .' To say (as far too many clergy say with bland irresponsibility) 'The Bible says . . .' is even harder.

The answer to this apparent difficulty is straightforward. We should not require the Bible to yield a consistent scheme of theology, in either of the Testaments, for that is not its function. Its function is to witness. It is for the church to provide theology or doctrine. The function of this body of testimony which we call the Bible is to be a norm of doctrine, not a system.

Chapter Eleven

The Bible as Norm and as the Church's Book

The best way to illustrate how the Bible can be used as a norm today is to give an example of using it in this way. If we take the subject of how we are to discover the true doctrine of God in the Bible, we cannot be accused of evading the issue with some easy or trivial example. We begin by reminding ourselves that we have emerged from the cosy atmosphere of the play school and laid aside the easy evasions of timid conservatism. Trying to sidle round the truth is not compatible with Christian faith. We must also remember that the fundamental category with which we shall be working is the Bible as witness, not as inspired oracle. This will sometimes mean balancing one part of the Bible against another, drawing up a kind of profit-and-loss account. For instance, we have to take account of the fact that the Bible both represents God as predestinating and asserts very clearly human responsibility for human actions. It also speaks freely of God's love and of God's wrath, without making any attempt to relate them to each other. One text speaks of us as 'partakers of the divine nature' (II Peter 1.4) but many others say that we can be partakers of the divine *life*. The two evangelists who describe the virginal conception of Jesus also include genealogies of Jesus which rest on the assumption that he was physically descended from Joseph. The accounts of the resurrection are in some places contradictory and confusing.

What we are seeking is the main impression made by the Bible in its witness to God's nature and being, the burden, the drift, what Irenaeus called the *hypothesis* and Tertullian the *ratio* and Athanasius the *skopos*. What is the impression left by the biblical record, the final picture given by the Bible, of God-in-Christ? It does not give us a picture of a deified man, a 'god-like man' (*theios anér*) such as the Hellenistic world was used to. It does not give us an account of two

Gods, a high God who is beyond suffering and a lower God who can do the requisite suffering for him, even though the first picture is very popular today and the second was always very attractive to the ancients. Nor can we honestly say that the Bible tells us of Jesus as a supremely good man who had no essential relation to God. What, in view of the career of Christ given in the New Testament, is God, the God whom we meet in the Old Testament, like? Does Christ make any serious difference to our understanding of God?

The Old Testament tells us that God is capable of acting in history: the book is full of historical narrative of different sorts, near-legendary, almost contemporary, or strongly ideological; the prophets are commentators upon the history that is happening around them; the apocalyptic parts are in a quite different mode also much concerned with God's activity in history. Clearly God is not compromised by encountering human existence and human experience. The anthropomorphic language, that is, language representing God as if he were a human being, which troubled the Rabbis and gave the Fathers of the early church great uneasiness, is not to be found only in the most primitive strata of the literature, but also in those parts of the Old Testament where thought about God is most advanced, such as the Book of Job and Second Isaiah. There is obviously no ontological barrier to God's action in the world, as the philosophers of the early church were always tempted to think. Again, the Old Testament says as clearly as possible that there is only one God. Other gods are, in the more ancient parts of the book, thought to exist but not to be comparable to the God of the Hebrew people, and in the later literature it is realized and proclaimed that no other gods exist, that anything else claiming to be divine is simply a no-god. The Old Testament also tells us that God can only be known by faith. This is not because it is difficult to recognize or encounter God; on the contrary, the writers of the Old Testament have for the most part no difficulty in knowing God in the sense of knowing that he exists. But he can only be known, in the sense that we know his character and his will, by faith. Second Isaiah and Job are quite clear about this; he is the sort of God who cannot be, as we today would say, mastered by scientific experiment nor explored by philosophic enquiry, just because he is so great, so transcendent (though not remote), so much master of human beings rather than open to being mastered by them. We can also learn from the Old Testament that God is a loving God; he loves his people, and this love, while it can be compared to the love of a mother for her child or of a husband for his wife, is more enduring than theirs; it is not vulnerable as theirs is (Hosea 11; Isa. 49.15).

When, having discovered this much about God's character from the Old Testament, we move to the New and look at what it says about the significance of Jesus Christ, we must first recognize the importance of eschatology. The message which Jesus proclaimed was certainly eschatological. This much is certain from the synoptic gospels. Protestant scholars have in the past found this embarrassing, especially those who at the end of the nineteenth and beginning of the twentieth century wished to build a christology purely on the teaching of Jesus allied with religious experience; Schleiermacher (much earlier, but their inspirer), Ritschl and Inge. They tried to ignore it altogether, to regard it as one of those Jewish integuments which the gospel was wrapped in when it reached us and which can be discarded. But eschatology is much too important an ingredient of the thought of the New Testament, and of the teaching of Jesus, for us to ignore it with any safety or integrity. The good news of the kingdom of God, or of heaven, was not the message of a wholly fulfilled eschatology, as Dodd once maintained; the kingdom had not completely come. Nor was it a wholly future event to be awaited by those who at the time of proclamation do not witness it, as Schweitzer suggested. Nor was it an indefinitely imminent event, as most conventional Christians today treat it, a kingdom which could come any minute these 50,000 years. Indefinite imminence is a contradiction in terms, and the proclaiming of an indefinitely imminent kingdom is a peculiarly futile procedure. The kingdom of God means an inaugurated but not consummated final time, last age. It certainly is here, proleptically, as it were, in a first instalment, but it has yet to be consummated. That is the eschatological note that runs through the whole of the New Testament, and it is consistent with the kind of apocalyptic to be found in the Book of Daniel and in much non-canonical Jewish literature of the period. And the thought that the kingdom of God has drawn near is consonant with the picture of God given in the Old Testament.

A prophet who arrives with a message announcing the last time or a Messiah who arrives and embodies the last time, is a highly Jewish concept. Jewish thought is not philosophical, metaphysical, but dynamic, historical, eschatological. To say that Jesus brings with him the last time is, in the Jewish mode, to attach to him unlimited significance. The writers of the New Testament do not all by any means describe Jesus as divine nor as God, but they do all, by subscribing to this eschatological interpretation of his meaning, confer on him an importance which is not clearly nor consistently defined, but which is unlimited.

The two greatest interpreters of the importance of Jesus in the New Testament, Paul and John, take markedly different lines. Paul's gospel is, of course, eschatological. We live 'between the cross and the end'; this conviction determines his ethics, his piety, everything. The last age has come, but is not yet consummated. Paul never directly calls Jesus God, though at Philippians 2.5–11 he comes close to doing so. For Jews such as Paul there could be only one God; and for Greeks (i.e. pagans) a thousand different gods of varying degrees. Paul attributes pre-existence to Christ, and if we conclude that Philippians 2.5–11 is not directly Pauline but is an already known Christian formula used by Paul, then Paul was not the first to speak of pre-existence in connection with Christ. He sees Christ as the Second Adam from heaven, as the Messiah in whom we are mystically incorporated, as he in whose death in a sense the whole human race died. He never defines in what sense Christ is a divine being; he was probably developing Jewish Hellenistic ideas which have otherwise disappeared. He has a strange and harrowing doctrine of the Messiah being made sin (II Cor. 5.21) and a curse (Gal. 3.13). His thought is intensely Jewish, but it also heralds the end of traditional Judaism. He gives us a glimpse of God involving himself in human affairs to the extent of suffering for us and with us, of the Messiah's death on the cross as a great *peripeteia*, master stroke, reversal of human expectation on the part of God, a righting of everything, that leaves us without rights but with new faith in God's mercy and God's providence. Paul has no doctrine of the incarnation; the church for him is not an extension of the incarnation, but the *locus* where Christ operates and is to be found. At one point he sums up Christianity in three words: 'Jesus, Spirit, Gospel' (II Cor. 11.4). How the Spirit comes in will be seen presently. He tells us directly surprisingly little about the teaching of Jesus, but he knows very well the character of Jesus. He speaks of his gentleness, his compassion, his refusal to please himself. He sees him above all as the representative of the love of God. Christ's sacrificial death commends God's love, as his resurrection demonstrates God's mysterious victory.

The Gospel according to St John represents the work of the other great theologian of the New Testament. It is a profound and authoritative interpretation of the significance of Jesus Christ rather than a straightforward report about his teaching and career. We cannot simply discard or condemn it as wholly unhistoric, but we must be constantly aware of the evangelist's interpretative intention. The late acceptance of the work into the canon should alone rule out its being written by John the Apostle, even if there were not plenty of signs that it comes at the end of the development of the thought of the New Testament. The efforts of J. A. T. Robinson to prove that it was written before AD 70, dear though they are to the hearts of many clergy who want to see the gospel vindicated as an authentic historical record, have won agreement from almost no other scholars and must be regarded as a *tour de force* rather than a serious contribution to the subject.

This gospel reads into the historical career of Jesus of Nazareth the church's gradually growing understanding of his significance. It reads back into his ministry the theological ideas which the best minds in the church had after some time arrived at. It may well give us some authentic information about his career; its spreading of the ministry over a longer period than two years is highly probable; the appearance by the Sea of Galilee described in the twenty-first chapter has a curious ring of truth about it. But what are we to make of a gospel which crams the resurrection, the ascension, the coming of the Holy Spirit and two appearances to the faithful in Jerusalem into a span of forty-eight hours? According to Matthew and Luke Jesus, when tempted in the desert, refused to turn stones into bread for the sake of creating a sensation. According to John within a few weeks he was turning water into wine for just those reasons. As we read the Fourth Gospel we must be aware of the fact that the author is capable of distorting or moulding historical facts for his own purposes and is recording the post-resurrection impression of Christ as if it were the pre-resurrection history. It was the Commentary on this gospel written by Hoskyns and Davey* which first brought this fact prominently forward to English-speaking readers, and in doing so they did New Testament criticism a great service.

St John's Gospel is not dominated by the kind of eschatological expectation which pervades most of the rest of the New Testament. It contains some apocalyptic language, enough to show that he is acquainted with that sort of vocabulary, but its fundamental interest is not eschatological in that sense. It effects with consummate skill the shift, evident elsewhere at the end of the first century and the beginning of the second, from eschatology to christology. It calls its readers to cease scanning the sky for signs of the spectacular End, and

*E. Hoskyns and F. N. Davey, *The Fourth Gospel*, London 1940.

instead to concentrate on the person and presence of Christ through the Spirit in the church now. This was not a sign of the Christian faith being overwhelmed by Hellenism but a necessary, unavoidable change of emphasis, without which Christianity might not perhaps have survived. John solves the eschatological problem which was then making itself felt, witness such passages as II Peter 3.1–10: why had Christ not come again? In his references to the Comforter (the Paraclete) he suggests without directly saying so that for most intents and purposes the coming of the Spirit is the *Parousia*, the 'Second Coming'. There will indeed be a consummation, a general resurrection, but meanwhile we must realize that the Redeemer is present in the church now, that he is acting now for salvation and for judgment. When the church in the middle of the second century accepted the Fourth Gospel into its canon it endorsed this doctrine, and has held to it ever since.

St John's Gospel pushes further than ever the doctrine of the pre-existence of Christ, and clarifies the position, going far to answer the question which Paul never clearly answered, what sort of divine being is Christ? Its answer appears in the *Logos*-doctrine, given in the first fourteen verses of the first chapter. This doctrine of Christ as the Word of God has, at least in terminology, affinities with Greek philosophy, but it is not a basically Greek answer. John's Logos-doctrine differs markedly from the Logos-doctrine of, for instance, Philo, the learned Jew of Alexandria who was a contemporary of St Paul. John also actually reaches a doctrine of incarnation towards which Paul's thought and perhaps Matthew's had been moving: 'the Word became flesh and dwelt among us . . .' (1.14). But it shows no sign at all of the idea, later evolved by the church, that Jesus Christ had two natures, a divine and a human.

We must control and balance this extraordinary document, the Fourth Gospel, with the witness to the historical Jesus given us by Matthew, Mark and Luke. In John Jesus is conscious of his own divinity and pre-existence and speaks almost incessantly on this theme. He is omniscient and knows that he is sinless. He can raise Lazarus from the tomb by a word and send his captors reeling back by simply speaking to them. He discourses philosophically with Pilate. In the synoptic gospels much material directly contradicts these assumptions. Jesus does not claim to be divine; on the contrary, when he says 'Why do you call me good? No one is good but God alone' (Mark 10.18) he implies that he is not God. He speaks relatively little about his own person and much about God and the message with which God has entrusted him. In the synoptics, for instance, Jesus describes God as a shepherd seeking his lost sheep; in John's gospel he says 'I am the good shepherd'. In the synoptics Jesus is pre-eminently a man of faith. His own faith is emphasized: he exhorts other to faith. In them he behaves as the Epistle to the Hebrews describes him, 'He learnt obedience by the things which he suffered' (5.8). All this is simply incompatible with a being who knows everything beforehand and who is by his constitution incapable of experiencing temptation or committing sin. In short, in the first three gospels Jesus, whatever else he may be, is wholly human, in John he is divine, and not quite human. But the Fourth Gospel never suggests that Jesus was incapable of suffering or dying and does not at all play down the significance of the Passion; on the contrary, Christ's suffering on the cross is the supreme moment of his glory. We conclude therefore that, though we may prefer to follow Paul and say that though Jesus Christ was in the form of God he did not count equality with God a thing to be grasped (Phil. 2.6), and envisage the Saviour as coming among us 'in a mystery', in a disguised form so that he was not recognized for what he was until after the resurrection (I Cor. 2.6–10), we cannot simply discard John's interpretation of Jesus. His is not, as it was for some time suspected to be, a Gnostic gospel. But it must be balanced by other witnesses in the New Testament.

The Holy Spirit makes almost no appearance in the synoptic gospels, but in John, the Acts and the epistles he rises like a sun. The key to the New Testament doctrine of the Spirit is that he is an eschatological phenomenon. He is God-at-the-end-of-the-world, a foretaste of heaven. He is not merely a kind of IOU of God's coming redemption, not just a trailer advertising celestial delights in the future, but an 'earnest' (*arrabōn*), a first instalment of salvation. He is the proof and guarantee of the unavoidableness of Christ, of his finality, of his ultimacy (should one say divinity?). The Spirit is deeply involved in the Christian experience of God. There are very few references to Christians praying, worshipping, prophesying or making decisions in the New Testament which do not mention the Holy Spirit. He is God in whom we return to God, the answer to the Old Testament's occasional and late sense of the inaccessibility of God. In Paul's doctrine we are bankrupt before God, but still can approach him confidently and joyfully because we can recognize him, know him and return to him in the Holy Spirit. The Spirit is also the bond between the church and the historical career of Jesus, in such a way that his career is not just a closed incident but in a sense is perpetually present to us. We are baptized into the Spirit; we celebrate the eucharist in the Spirit. In a word, the Spirit is God who is sovereign over time.

This is the way in which we assemble the raw material from the Bible to prepare for the Christian doctrine of God. The doctrine has still to be wrought into the traditional doctrine of the Trinity achieved by the church only after three hundred years' discussion and controversy, trial and error. We cannot here follow that story. But we can note some points which have emerged in this exercise of using the Bible as a norm. First, we have certainly not used all the material available in the Bible, whether Old or New Testaments. No system or approach has ever been able to do this nor ever could, and it was by trying by illegitimate means to use every verse of the Bible in aid of their theologies that interpreters in the past have fallen into illusion about the Bible. We have tried to select that which is salient, significant, creative and as far as possible consistent. Next, we have run away from no critical problem, forced no evidence to witness to that which it does not witness to. On the contrary, we have, as far as possible, made critical scholarship our ally and not our enemy. Finally, we have used the text of the Bible, not as oracle, not as ready-made manual of doctrine, but strictly as witness, evidence. And we have attempted, sketchily and in a short compass, to sum up this evidence, to strike the right balance, to seek out the main burden or impress of the whole, as a judge might treat evidence when he is addressing a jury. This, we believe, is the correct way to use the Bible as a norm. It allows no short cuts, no simple solutions. But in the end it leaves us with the fairest and most authentic presentation of the biblical evidence, and one which we can most confidently trust.

II

We must observe that the Bible, whatever its merits or demerits, is in the strictest sense indispensable to the existence of Christianity. Without it, our knowledge of ancient Judaism and of the origins of Christianity, would be reduced to almost nothing. We would be left with an early and very bare creed, two sacraments and the practice of prayer and worship, but would have no idea of their significance. Christianity is an historical religion in that it claims that God revealed himself in the history of the chosen race and the career of the Messiah who arose from that race. If we did not possess the Bible our prime source of knowledge for that history and that career would be lost.

There are no substitutes for the Bible, for every suggested substitute depends in the end on the Bible. When *Essays and Reviews* (see above p. 39) was published, Newman remarked in a letter to a friend that the basis of the religion of the Protestants was now destroyed, but that the Catholic Church was unaffected because it could rely on tradition. This was nonsense, as the history of the next hundred years proved. No tradition can take the place of the Bible, which is in fact the vital, indispensably canonized early tradition of the church. No creed can be a substitute, because though a case can be made for saying that the earliest form of the Apostles' Creed in its historical descent is independent of the Bible, it is so skeletonic and uninformative as to be of very little use as early tradition. The 'Rule of Faith', which was recognized by some writers in the second and third centuries, was no more than a summary of what the church at that time was preaching, and the writers themselves attempt to prove it from the Bible. It is indeed true that the church has been preaching and teaching from the earliest times continuously in a line of doctrine formally independent of the Bible. But if we ask, What was the church preaching and teaching at the earliest period?, there is only one source to which we can go for information, and that is the Bible. Between us and the historical careers of Jesus and his apostles stands immovably the Bible.

Not only is the Bible indispensable as a source. It is also indispensable as a norm. It is easy, but undesirable, to treat the Bible simply as a starting-point for Christian doctrine, as, for instance, Newman did in his *Essay on the Development of Christian Doctrine*. It was sufficient for him if any later development of doctrine could find *some* justification, no matter how tenuous, in scripture; he could then claim that it started there, no matter how luxuriously it developed later. But this is to fly in the face of Catholic tradition. Every early Father of the church, and every mediaeval writer up to at least the fourteenth century, knew and taught that the Bible was the norm for Christian doctrine, that against which Christian doctrine must be measured, no matter how odd might be their methods of measuring. If the Bible is not a norm, then Christianity is afloat chartless on a wide sea of doctrine. There is no other conceivable basic, primary norm, though there must be secondary norms. It is not enough to say that what the authorities of the church determine is the norm because they have the sole right to determine so. The history of mediaeval Christianity in the West is enough to refute this idea. That orthodox, Catholic Christianity is committed to the Bible as a norm there should be no doubt.

In fact it is not difficult to determine the true status and authority of the Bible, even when we reject the oracular view or the fundamentalist view of its nature. The Bible's status and authority rest on its function as witness, as testimony. Under this category we can unite virtually all its contents. The Book of Genesis is witness to the ancient Jewish understanding of God in relation to creation and mankind and civilization. Exodus begins the story of God's relation to history. The Law books in a multitude of diverse ways testify to the Jewish conception of God in relation to ethics, personal, domestic, social and national. The historical books witness to the history of the chosen people, and witness all the more honestly because they testify to the failure and back-sliding of that people as well as to its faithfulness and obedience to God. The historical value of the Books of Chronicles is small, but they play their part as theological interpretation of history in post-Exilic Judaism. The Psalms witness to the spirituality of the Jewish people, and this in its turn throws light on their conception of God. The Wisdom literature in its own way witnesses to the ethical ideas of the ancient Jews, and as they were orientated almost wholly towards their God they do not take the form of ethical theories such as we find in Plato or among the Stoics but in a long list of rules of thumb. What matters is obeying God's will, not counting and analysing virtues. The prophetic literature does not consist in a series of mysterious predictions of events far in the future but in comments by a series of prophets, many of them anonymous, on the history of Israel from the eighth to the fourth century BC by commentators who were contemporaries of the events upon which they were commenting. That the New Testament consists of a series of testimonies to the career and significance of Jesus Christ regarded as the climax of all history, Jewish or other, needs no demonstration. In short, if we regard the Bible as a book of witness to the character and activity of God unfolded over many centuries and culminating in the appearance of Jesus Christ, we shall at last reach a just appreciation of its true status and authority.

Now if we consider the nature of witness or testimony, we shall see that it need not be infallible nor guaranteed to be exempt from error; indeed it is absurd to imagine that it should be so. Think of a body of testimony collected by the prosecution in a criminal trial. If the prosecutor claimed that his evidence was guaranteed to be inerrant before he set it before the jury, nobody would believe him. Testimony depends upon its own inherent power of conviction, not on a claim to infallibility.

Again, a body of witness or evidence can very well be much varied in character, in relevance and in accuracy, and still perform its proper function well enough. This can apply to the evidence given in a trial, not all of which is necessarily either relevant or convincing and some of which can be unreliable or false without affecting the whole. This is even more true of a book describing some great event embodying the witness of several different people, like John Hersey's remarkable book about the explosion of the atomic bomb, *Hiroshima* (1986). No doubt some of the details in this account are inaccurate and some passages are inconsistent with others, but this does not invalidate the powerful effect of the whole.

What matters in any collection of evidence or testimony is the impression or burden or total effect of the compilation. This is precisely what the jury, assisted by the judge, in a trial has to determine; not, is every detail infallibly true? But, what is the impression left by the whole? Apply all these considerations to the Bible, making allowance that the Bible is much more varied in its literary forms, and is concerned with a much longer period of time, than any example which we have given. You will then see that when we determine that the proper category to allot to the Bible is that of witness we preserve its relevance and force and significance without finding it necessary to treat it in an oracular fashion nor apply to it the unreal and indefensible epithets of inerrant or infallible.

The question can of course now be asked, 'What has become of the doctrine of the inspiration of the Bible?' The only honest answer must be that it has disappeared. The doctrine of inspiration in its traditional form was always unreal and unworkable. It was a compliment paid to the Bible rather than a serious estimate of its nature. Any other definition of the inspiration of the Bible, e.g. that it is inspired because it is inspiring, either does not apply to the whole book or is so different from the traditional doctrine that it is dishonest to call it by the same name. In place of the old unreal and confusing names of inspiration and inerrancy we must substitute those of uniqueness and sufficiency. No collection of documents can possibly rival the Bible in importance. And the evidence there collected, though not infallible, is sufficient for conveying conviction. That is all that we should ask of the Bible.

Finally, we should face the question whether this argument has not reduced the Bible to a collection of diverse ancient documents, and no more, like Nennius' *History of Britain* or the collection of Theodosius the Deacon. Certainly the Bible is a collection of ancient documents whose literary form, language, style and accuracy is no greater nor more than the best of the periods in which they were written, and in some cases less than that. What gives to the Bible its unique significance and power and its perennial freshness is nothing else than its subject. What it witnesses to is what gives it life and permanence, not the manner in which it witnesses. The Bible always has had and always will have a life-giving and stimulating effect upon its readers because it witnesses to life which is life indeed. It witnesses to the character and activity of God through the medium of entirely human witnesses and writers. It is not an oracle; it is not inerrant. But it imparts life and power because it witnesses to life and power.

III

All that we have written so far leads inevitably to the question which we have so far approached indirectly sometimes but not yet faced: what is the relation of the Bible to the church? Two quite different, indeed polar, positions have been taken here at various times and by various people during the course of Christian history.

　1. The Bible is independent of the church, autonomous, self-sufficient, needing no interpreter, no intermediary between it and the individual Christian. The Anglican divine William Chillingworth (1602 – 1644) coined the slogan 'the Bible, and the Bible alone, is the religion of Protestants' (though he later receded somewhat from that position). Others have spoken of 'the Bible without notes' or of the Bible not seen through the spectacles of the creeds. The Westminster Confession of 1643 apparently takes this attitude, though it also endorses cheerfully some traditional creeds. And innumerable Protestant sects declare and believe that they teach the 'four-square gospel' or the simple gospel, the pure doctrine of the Bible unsullied by interpretation or creed or tradition.

　One can understand many Christians in the circumstances of the sixteenth century imagining that they could return or had returned to the doctrine of the Bible unassisted by any traditional interpretation. They saw the necessity of abandoning many doctrines and practices of the late mediaeval Western church, and of reforming many others. And the standard by which they carried out this pruning process was certainly to be found in the Bible. Some of the Reformed traditions, such as the Lutheran and the Anglican, consciously recognized that they were not returning simply to the Bible, but to the Bible as it was understood and interpreted in the early centuries of the church's existence.

But, whatever may have been thought four hundred years ago, the ideal of purely biblical doctrine without any interpretation or tradition is an impossible dream, and those sects who imagine that they have achieved this ideal are simply deceiving themselves, and their theologians (if they have any) are clearly incompetent. The church wrote the Bible. The Bible did not descend from heaven (as the Mormons' Bible is alleged to have done), and in deciding the canon the church decided the limits of the Bible. The Bible does not interpret itself. It is not a cassette-recording with a commentary. Most of its doctrine is not self-evident, self-explanatory, blindingly obvious. The history of Christian thought (to which the sects pay very little attention) shows that there are innumerable different ways of interpreting the Bible. It has not produced *eo ipso* automatic agreement among Christians. The Ecumenical Movement, which has succeeded in showing that many Christians have much more in common with each other doctrinally than they previously thought they had, is not founded simply on the Bible, but on the Bible as interpreted by the Nicene Creed, i.e. on the developed tradition of the first few centuries of the church's life. Further, the Bible not only does not preach itself, it does not perpetuate itself, copy itself, print and circulate itself either. It needs the church for that. In short, the Bible demands, needs and implies an interpreting community. The whole concept of a New Testament entails ineluctably a church to use it, preach it, teach it and therefore of course to interpret it. The Bible needs the church, and is, if not incomplete, at least dumb without it.

2. The other position, polar as we have said to the first, on the subject of the relation of the Bible to the church is to state that the Bible is the possession of the church and consequently the church can control the Bible. The church made the canon, the Bible belongs entirely to the church, and the church is entitled to withhold or suppress the Bible in part or whole, if it thinks fit, merely informing the faithful what it is that the Bible teaches. They can accept this on the faith of the church. They do not need to work out for themselves the true message of the Bible, indeed most of them are incapable of doing so. Such a position was in fact that of the church of the Counter-Reformation. This attitude to the Bible is also consonant with the idea that in the last resort the church does not need the Bible, because the church has another source of revealed truth, it has tradition. The Protestants may involve themselves in inextricable labyrinths of doubt and uncertainty by indulging in criticism of the Bible. The Catholics can view their antics with a superior smile,

secure in the possession of tradition. The private individual has no right to his own interpretation of the Bible, no capacity to exercise such a right, and had better not be let loose on the Bible.

We hasten to say that the extreme form of this second position which we have outlined would find very few supporters in the contemporary Roman Catholic Church. In fact, a remarkable renewal of interest in and study of the Bible has taken place in that communion since the Second Vatican Council. We must also point out that there is this much truth in the second position: that the Bible is a large, complex and diverse book, and that to let the uninstructed reader try to derive his doctrine from it is likely to result, and has time and time again resulted, in folly and manifest error. One has only to look at the religious ideas of that super-individualist, that theological solipsist, General Charles Gordon, to see that. And we are not confident that the practice much indulged in nowadays of encouraging people who know nothing of the background and composition of the Bible to fly to it for all their religious needs and to find the answers to all doubts and difficulties in it is an entirely sound one.

But when all is said and done, it must be admitted that this second account of the relation of the Bible to the church is quite as untenable as the first. It is a basic fact that as far as doctrine is concerned the church without the Bible is rudderless and chartless. How do we know what the church is and where it came from? If the church in effect says, 'you must accept my teaching as true on the strength of my word', we are entirely justified in asking, 'What, then are your credentials? Why should we trust you in this way?' The church has perfectly good credentials. They are the Bible. The Bible gives us the pedigree of the church and guarantees its authority, not vice versa. Between us and the origins of Christianity the Bible stands immovably. No appeal to tradition, no invocation of the church's authority, can change this fact.

It is quite clear that the theologians of the first thousand years of the history of the church, both in the East and the West, regarded the Bible as a norm by which Christian doctrine was to be judged, not just as a base from which doctrine was to start, and not just as one alternative of two equally authentic sources of doctrine. If any proposition is supported by unanimous catholic tradition this one is. The church is not in a position to suppress or supersede or modify the Bible. It is not the master of the Bible, but its interpreter, not its controller but its guardian. Therefore the second of these two ideas of the relation of the Bible to the church is as unacceptable as the first.

It is not difficult to outline in theory the proper relationship of the Bible to the church. The old saw attributed to Provost Hawkins of Oriel College, Oxford, about 1820 puts it in a nutshell: 'The church to teach and the Bible to prove.' This has in fact been the principle upon which, not merely the Church of England, but the Church Catholic has operated for the greater part of its history. 'Trust the church and shut your eyes' has never been the traditional method of teaching the Bible. The church commends the Bible to the enquirer or believer so that he can see for himself that what the church teaches is true. Unrestricted individual interpretation of the Bible by the uninstructed usually results in folly. But the Christian body which is afraid to let the faithful see that what it teaches is in accordance with the Bible draws upon itself the suspicion that it knows its teaching to be non-scriptural or extra-scriptural. The individual Christian must be allowed the opportunity to see for himself or herself. This does not preclude the church from encouraging the faithful to make use of all possible authentic means of understanding the Bible, and profiting from more than a century's methodical study and analysis of it. In fact, the church has a duty to do this, and sometimes is negligent of this duty. But the idea that the Christian must somehow be protected from the Bible or must take as sole doctrinal *pabulum* the church's teaching and not the Bible is utterly wrong.

Chapter Twelve

In Praise of the Bible

We have been obliged to spend a lot of time in this book showing what the Bible is not, dissipating illusions, puncturing inflated claims, so that we are in danger of giving the impression that we have a low view of the Bible or that it is 'just like any other book'. But this would be a totally false conclusion. We have indeed already shown how essential a place the Bible holds in the structure of the Christian faith and how indispensable it is a basis for our knowledge of Christianity. But we follow this up by a section in appreciation of the Bible, because there is so much in it to love and admire.

Many readers will be acquainted with *The Literary Guide to the Bible* edited by Robert Alter and Frank Kermode (1988). This is intended for those who wish to read the Bible as literature and not as a spiritual source-book. We have already pointed out (see pp. 97–98 above) that the Bible is not written for purely literary purposes, but there can be no doubt but that some parts of the Bible do constitute literature of a very high order. Here are some of the literary merits of the Bible.

We may well begin with Genesis 1.1–2.3. We have here a solemn, dignified, immensely impressive account of the creation of the world. As we have seen, it is not scientifically accurate, but it does convey with superb effect the creative activity of God, the all-important fact that God made the world good, not evil, and that the human race is the crown of his creation. As we read on through Genesis, we meet in chapters 37–47 (excluding chapter 38) the story of Joseph. This is a traditional theme beautifully adapted to fit the life of the patriarch. It is story-telling at its highest, with plenty of scope for emotion without ever straying into sentimentality. Small wonder that it has been the theme of later works, from the long novel by Thomas Mann, *Joseph and His Brethren*, to the musical, 'Joseph and His Amazing Technicolour Dreamcoat' by Tim Rice and Andrew Lloyd Webber.

In the historical books we have two ancient songs. The first is

Judges 5.2–31, Deborah's triumph song over the defeat of Sisera. The second is David's lament over the death of Saul and Jonathan in II Samuel 1.19–27. This may very well have been composed by David himself. These are two admirable examples of early Hebrew poetry. In what is called the 'Succession Narrative' we have the story of Absalom's rebellion (II Sam. 13–19). Here is another extremely successful example of story-telling, this time based on solid history. Dialogue and character are admirably depicted. It is like a very effective historical novel, and is far more interesting than most historical novels.

Before we leave the historical section of the Old Testament, we ought to notice Nehemiah's narrative. There is no reason not to regard this as genuine autobiographical reminiscence. In particular the description of Nehemiah's nocturnal ride round the ruins of Jerusalem narrated in Nehemiah 2 is justly famous and has often been portrayed by artists.

The prophets for the most part uttered their oracles in verse. In trying to understand their messages we must never forget that we are reading poetry. The Hebrew syntactical verse structure can very often be traced even in translation. Some of the prophets were poets of no small ability as well as speakers on behalf of God, and merely to read their work is to enjoy the pleasure of reading great poetry. Perhaps no prophet had more imagination than Hosea: his work is constantly illuminated with vivid scenes or references to the details of the countryside of Northern Israel. Read for example chapters 6 and 7 and notice how many scenes he conjures up: rain, morning dew, a butcher at work, a band of murderers in ambush, a burglar breaking into a house, a baker at his oven, a silly dove caught in a net, priests of Baal gashing themselves in order to court the god's favour, a treacherous bow. Or turn from Hosea to the anonymous prophet of the exile: his opening chords in Isaiah 40 are among the most glorious passages in the Bible; and he maintains his lofty style throughout, reaching his literary climax perhaps in chapter 52 with his moving call to Zion to awake from her misery and put on robes suitable for her triumphant return from exile.

When we turn to the Writings, the third section of the Hebrew Bible, we find no scarcity of literary achievement. Some of the Psalms are unequalled in their effective expression of Israel's devotion whether it be the beautiful harvest psalm (Ps. 65), or the hymn is praise to God's creation (Ps. 104), or the lovely psalm of trust in God (Ps. 121). We can only briefly mention these, but there are many more of equal beauty. The Book of Job is a narrative poem (chs 3–42.6) with a prose prologue and epilogue. Like Hosea the author of Job has a powerful imagination and illuminates his message by means of countless images and scenes drawn from contemporary life. Consider for example Job's pathetic lament at the ephemeral nature of man's existence (Job 14), or his realistic description of social ills in chapter 24, or the beautiful chapter 28 in praise of wisdom, which comes as an *entr'acte* between the end of the friends' arguments and Job's last great challenge to God in chapters 29–31. But above all read chapters 38–39, the beginning of God's reply to Job, in which God dwells upon the greatness and incomprehensibility of his creation in order to convince Job of his unfitness to argue with God.

Three other books among the Writings must be mentioned for their literary excellence. The author of the Book of Daniel, the latest book in the Old Testament, has succeeded remarkably in conveying the majesty and transcendence of God, who is represented as the real force behind history, despite the foolish pretensions of worldly rulers. Perhaps his *tour de force* comes in chapter 5, the story of Belshazzar's feast. This is not historical at all, but gives us an unforgettable picture of the futility of worldly glory when compared with the purposes of God. The second of these books is the Book of Ruth, a lovely pastoral idyll cast in the almost legendary time of the Judges. And the third is the Book of Jonah, a critique of the exclusive Judaism of the post-exilic period, in which Jonah represents Judaism. The author must have had a keen sense of humour, as he describes Jonah in 4.1–5 as saying in effect to God, 'I knew your fatal weakness, your tendency to have mercy. It was because I did not want you to have mercy on Nineveh that I tried to flee to Tarshish'.

One does not at first sight tend to regard any part of the New Testament as a candidate for high literary honours, but in fact there are passages of great literary value in the New Testament. The Gospel of Mark as a whole is written in a very simple Greek, almost ungrammatical at times, but the total effect is deeply moving. It is not surprising that people flock to hear a really competent actor simply reciting the Gospel of Mark. If ever one has to introduce Christianity to a complete newcomer, it is an excellent idea to ask him or her to read Mark through at one sitting. The gospel reaches its literary climax in the passion story in 14.32–15.39. There is not an unnecessary word; there is no dwelling on the agony of the crucifixion. Mark never approaches within a hundred miles of sentimentality. The whole narrative shows a classical economy of detail, but it is amazingly effective in conveying the awful importance of what is happening.

Paul was a complete master of Hellenistic Greek. He never writes for literary effect, but for that very reason can be very effective from a literary point of view. Most famous of all is his description of love in I Corinthians 13: but we should not forget his moving climax in Philippians 3.11 in the words 'that if possible I may attain the resurrection from the dead'; or his indignant account of what he has suffered in the course of his mission in II Corinthians 11.21–29. It is difficult to separate one's theological appreciation from one's literary appreciation, but surely I Peter 2.1–10 is one of the most beautiful parts of the New Testament with its profound exposition of the nature of the church, expressed to a large extent in language borrowed from the Old Testament's description of the vocation of Israel.

Now we must try to evaluate the Bible as a holy book, the scriptures of one of the great world religions. Here we encounter a great virtue of the Bible which is perhaps not so obvious in the scriptures of some other religions, its down-to-earth quality. When living among predominantly rural Christians in South India we found this down-to-earthness of the Bible was specially appreciated. Students reading Hosea's condemnation of Israel's forms of idolatry could look across the fields and see very similar rites being carried out. The Indian village wife, living in a one-room mud house thatched with palmyra leaves, would know exactly what it meant when the woman who had lost the coin proceeded to sweep out the house: it meant sweeping out that one room. The Bible never loses touch with daily life and if one lives in a largely pre-industrial environment one fits very easily into the world of the Bible. To this we can add another quality, the honesty of the Bible. By this we do not mean that the scriptures of other religions are dishonest. Certainly not. But the Bible impresses one by the extremely honest and realistic picture it gives of the people of God, whether in the Old Testament or the New. Early Christian writers often accuse the Jews of being a peculiarly stubborn and disobedient people. But this accusation is made on the basis of the writings of the prophets, which the Israelites preserved and honoured despite the many condemnations of Israel which their works contain. The same thing could be said on a smaller scale of the New Testament writers. Paul describes the church in Corinth as 'sanctified in Christ Jesus, called to be saints', but he makes no attempt to hide the grievous sinfulness of some Corinthian Christians; and in II Corinthians he protests most bitterly at the outrageous way in which they have treated him. The Corinthian church itself had the courage to preserve these letters, even though they reflected so unpleasantly on their own community; and so the Pauline letters became part of the Christian scriptures. The same could be said of the letter to the Galatians. As well as realism, we can certainly attribute honesty to the writers of the Bible. They were not afraid to face the facts.

More perhaps than anything else is the Bible to be valued for its devotional use. This is not of course to be entirely divorced from its function as record and as basis and norm of Christian doctrine. The Bible has been through the ages and still is the daily support, bread of life, iron ration, never-failing standby of Christians in all circumstances. It has maintained Christians in illness, in bereavement, in disaster, in persecution, in perplexity. Wise Christians use it daily. When a Christian is in prison, whether through his own fault or through the wickedness of others, the first thing he will ask for is a Bible. Here is the testimony of Pastor Hans Lilje, imprisoned by Hitler during the last war, deprived of any reading matter whatever: 'Under these circumstances, I could only repeat passages from the Bible, and verses from the hymn-book, which I had retained in my memory. How grateful I am to all my teachers who had made me learn by heart hymns and poems, Greek lyrics, Latin odes and Hebrew psalms! They provided me with a treasure which in those hard days was literally priceless.'* With the decline of classical learning we can hardly be expected to learn Greek lyrics and Latin odes. But that children should be required to learn passages from the Bible by heart should surely form a part of the education of every child of committed Christian parents. Here also is the witness of a still more modern prisoner. Roger Augue, a Frenchman, was held hostage in Lebanon for almost a year, being released in November 1987. He writes as follows: 'I am sure that it was God who set me free. The Palestinian guard who gave me a Bible did me a blessed service. I prayed every day and learned the Psalms in English by heart. Being able to read the Bible kept me sane'.†

But how shall we use the Bible as our daily fare? Not all parts of it are equally suitable. It would be an ingenious soul who could get much spiritual nourishment from the Book of Esther or Ecclesiastes. We must of course exercise discretion: many parts of the Old Testament are virtually useless for this purpose, but not of course the

*Quoted in E. A. Blackburn (ed.) *A Treasury of the Kingdom*, Oxford 1954, p. 144.
†Quoted in the Bible Society's publication *Word in Action*, Summer 1988.

Psalms. Notice how both those prisoners referred to them. Read
Psalm 63, for example, or Psalm 84, or Psalm 91, or Psalm 139. All
provide incomparable material for meditation and mental recall
throughout the day. Or turn to the anonymous prophet of the exile
and read, for instance, Isaiah 43.1–4:

> Fear not, for I have redeemed you;
> I have called you by your name, you are mine . . .
> Because you are precious in my eyes,
> and honoured, and I love you.

Who can despair if he has such assurances as these?

The New Testament is naturally the place *par excellence* from which
the Christian draws daily nourishment. Many are the ways that men
and women of prayer have recommended for making the best use of it.
A good plan is to take a gospel, preferably perhaps one of the first
three, and go through it incident by incident, imagining that you were
present. Be one of those who heard Jesus say to Jairus' daughter
'Little lamb (the literal translation of *Talitha* in Mark 5.41) get up'. Or
put yourself in the place of the father of the epileptic boy in Mark
9.24, and exclaim with him: 'I believe – help my unbelief!'. Or take an
extract from Jesus' teaching as recorded in the Sermon on the Mount.
'Blessed are the pure in heart, for they shall see God' (Matt. 5.8).
There is enough material there for a lifetime's meditation. Or take one
of Jesus' vivid parables, especially as recorded by Luke, the scene for
example of the man who comes knocking up his neighbour at mid-
night in order to borrow a loaf (11.5f.). We seem to be transported
straight into rural Galilee in Jesus' time; translate it into current event.

Paul's writings are alive with passages which speak to us directly
across the centuries, and which seem specifically written in order to
enable us to stand firm in adversity. Read II Corinthians 1.3–7, for
example; what a magnificent exposition of the nature of Christian
hope! Or turn to Romans 8.31–39 for a memorable expression of faith
in face of all sorts of opposition. One might recommend the whole of
Philippians as material suitable for our daily bread. Almost every
sentence can be applicable to our circumstances today. Or, for the
matter of that, we might equally turn to Paul's disciple who wrote
Ephesians and allow ourselves to be built up by his lofty description of
the Christian's status and privileges, and of what it means to live in the
world as a committed member of the church. Hebrews might seem at
first sight rather obscure or complicated for the ordinary Christian.
But read Hebrews 5.7–10 for an incomparable sketch of the full

humanity of Jesus; or turn to 12.1–2 for an exposition of what it means to share in the communion of saints. I Peter 4.12–19 was written for Christians encountering persecution and is just as relevant today as when it was first written. The same could be said of the Book of Revelation – except that you do not need to wait till persecution comes along in order to benefit from it. All Christians in all circumstances can benefit from reading that splendid vision of the risen Lord in Revelation 1.12–20: 'Fear not: I am the first and the last and he who lives; I was dead and behold I am alive for ever and ever. And I hold the keys of death and of what comes after death' (our translation).

We have only given a few almost random examples from an inexhaustible treasury. Suffice it to say that as a source of spiritual comfort, strength, and encouragements the Bible is incomparable. Every Christian who can read should avail himself or herself of this means of unfailing daily bread.

Christians should therefore show respect for the Bible. This does not mean that we should keep it under the aspidistra in the front room, but that we should not misuse it. We have already suggested some ways by which the Bible is misused; trying to make it foretell our future, for instance, or treating it as if it was a crossword puzzle. But there are other ways also. Some years ago a dean of an Anglican cathedral was preaching at a choral festival. He took as his text a half-verse from the Book of Lamentations in the King James Version. It ran 'I am their music' (Lam. 3.63b). The theme of his discourse was that God should be the music of our lives, etc. Now in fact the preacher in selecting this text had only consulted a concordance. He had not troubled himself to look the verse up in its context; still less had he consulted a modern translation. Had he done both of these essential tasks for anyone who takes the Bible seriously he would have discovered that the correct translation of this half-verse is: 'I am the burden of their songs.' The author, far from thinking in terms of God as the music of our lives, complains that he is the subject of his enemy's mocking songs. To treat the Bible in this way is to show it disrespect. The responsible Christian should not only use the Bible; he should respect it and honour its authors. Without them there would have been no Judaism and no Christianity.

But when all necessary safeguards for preserving a care for the context of any biblical passage have been accepted, we still must face the fact that some biblical texts always have been, and no doubt always will be, used and quoted out of their context and that some of them live, as it were, beyond their context. We are not here referring to a 'plenary sense' (*sensus plenior*) supposed to be open to discovery beneath the apparent literal sense of the text. This 'plenary sense' is a complete illusion and belongs to the obsolete world of allegorizing the Bible. What is here intended is the manifest fact that many texts of the Bible are used and exercise powerful influence beyond their immediate historical contexts. When we find the opening verses of Second Isaiah's great work, 'Comfort ye, comfort ye, my people . . .' (Isa. 40.1) sung in Handel's *Messiah*, they are certainly being used well beyond their context, as are the words of the last and greatest of the 'Servant Songs' when they occur in the same oratorio. Countless passages from the Psalms and many of our Lord's parables (e.g. the 'Go thou and do likewise' of the parable of the Good Samaritan; Luke 10.29–37), the majority of the sayings attributed to Jesus in all four gospels, many passages in St Paul (e.g. I Cor. 13, and Rom. 8.31–39), and some striking sayings in Revelation, are constantly used and quoted with almost no reference to their context. It would be absurd to refuse legitimacy to this kind of use of biblical texts.

But we can reasonably distinguish and impose some limits to this treatment of the Bible. The extra-contextual use must have some proper connection with the textual use. As an example of illegitimate extra-contextual use, we may take the quotation from the Book of Job placed at the beginning of the Order for the Burial of the Dead in the English *Book of Common Prayer*. In the Prayer Book it runs: 'I know that my Redeemer liveth, and that he shall stand at the latter day upon the earth: and though after my skin worms destroy this body, yet in my flesh shall I see God, whom I shall see for myself, and mine eyes behold, and not another' (Job 19.25–27). In this version, the passage is a striking prophecy in the Old Testament of the resurrection of the body at the Second Coming of Christ. But the passage fares very differently in the hands of a modern translator, better informed than the men of the sixteenth century. The Revised Standard Version runs: 'But in my heart I know that my vindicator lives and that he will rise at last to speak in court: and I shall discern my witness standing at my side and see my defending counsel, even God himself.' In this rendering all that Job is saying is that in the end God will vindicate him. The reference to 'flesh' has disappeared and is buried under a footnote which says 'probable reading, Hebrew unintelligible'. This is an honest treatment of the passage. Both the Revised Standard Version and the Jerusalem Bible try to retain some reference to a future life in the verses, wrongly, in our opinion, because Job on more than one occasion declares roundly that after death man (unlike nature) has no future life, no awakening. In this instance the desire of Christian interpreters to read Christian doctrine into the Old Testament by hook or by crook has overcome common sense and sound scholarship.

But we can find one modern example of an extra-contextual quotation from Job which is eminently proper. When the Jews set up a memorial at Belsen to those of their race who had been ruthlessly murdered in huge numbers by the merciless minions of the Nazi regime in Germany they inscribed on it the stark words: 'O earth, cover not my blood, And let my cry find no resting-place' (Job 16.18). Nothing could be more appropriate than the application of Job's protest against the unjust treatment which he believes that he has received to the protest of all humanity against the unspeakable horror of this crime.

An interesting testing-ground of the distinctions which we have been making here is provided by Charles Wesley's exquisite hymn, 'Come, O thou Traveller unknown'. This, as is well known, takes the story of Jacob wrestling with an angel (Gen. 32.22–32) and reinter- prets it as the Christian wrestling with God in prayer. Is this legitimate? The story originally derives from a legend of a hero wrestling with a river-god, just as Achilles has to fight against a river-god in the *Iliad*; but it was used, perhaps a little later, as an aetiological legend told to explain why the Israelites are ritually forbidden to eat a particular part of an animal. Later still this very old tale was spiritualized to explain why Jacob was called Israel, and the place Peniel or Penuel: he had in some sense seen God. So far the Old Testament brings us. But Charles Wesley gives it a Christian interpretation. This is a picture of the Christian gradually realizing in prayer the boundless love of God declared in Christ. Into his interpretation he weaves several other Old Testament references, also Christianized:

> Thyself has called me by thy Name,
> Look on thy hands and read it there

is a reminiscence of Isaiah 49.16, 'Behold, I have graven you on the palms of my hands', but also of course an allusion to Christ's hands nailed to the cross. And 'the morning breaks, the shadows flee' refers to Song of Solomon 2.17 and 4.6 'until the morning break and the shadows flee'. This is not, as Origen, the ancient Fathers and the mediaevals would have thought it, a mystic prediction made in the dim past and miraculously fulfilled thousands of years later. It is a beautiful piece of poetic reinterpretation of the passage in Genesis made in the light of Christian experience. And we can allow it as legitimate because it faithfully maintains and expands the original theme for which the Jewish writers had used the elements of the ancient legends, that is the knowledge of God. In Christ we can now see God, know his character and his will, more fully than ever Jacob did at Peniel.

We must therefore allow the extra-contextual interpretation of the Bible, the interpretation of it beyond its immediate context. But this license will only apply to parts of the Bible. We cannot imagine the precept 'Thou shalt not suffer a witch to live' (Ex. 22.18) nor the unsavoury story of Ehud and Eglon the King of Moab (Judg. 3.15–30) yielding any such fuller meaning. Perhaps such a process can only be applied to the high spots of the Old Testament. Even in the New Testament it would be absurd to try to find a fuller meaning in the genealogies of Jesus, nor in pseudo-Paul's injunction to Timothy to drink wine for medical purposes (I Tim. 5.23). And even the fuller meaning must have a proper and reasonable connection with the original passage in its context. We must never allow our fuller, extra-contextual, treatment of any passage to spill over into allegory. The essence of allegorizing is that the original, natural connection between the passage and its meaning is broken and arbitrary interpretation steps in. Christianity is a religion indissolubly linked with history. We must not be afraid of maintaining this principle in our interpretation of the Bible.

One other point about reading the Bible is relevant here. It is a great advantage to have a modern translation. We have already pointed out that there is a wide variety of modern translations available in English. One sometimes encounters a resistance to modern translations on the part of those who are deeply attached to the King James, or Authorized Version, of 1611, especially when it is a question of reading the Bible in public worship: 'It sounds better than modern versions do.' It is certainly true that the King James Version was composed at a time when English was capable of immense heights and depths. After all Shakespeare was a contemporary of the King James Version translators. But Shakespeare is not always very intelligible even on the stage, and neither is the King James Version. Another objection to the King James Version is that it was an excellent translation *in its time*. But since it was published we have learned a great deal about the manuscripts of the New Testament, and it is plain that the Greek manuscripts that the translators used for the New

Testament were later and inferior compared with what is available now. Add to this that our knowledge of biblical Hebrew and New Testament Greek has grown considerably in the last four hundred and fifty years. There are many places where we now know that the KJV translators were mistaken in their rendering of the original. One suspects that this attachment to the KJV has got more nostalgia than common sense about it.

But if one uses a modern translation it is a good precaution when studying the Bible to use more than one. Recent modern translations are inspired by a desire not only to translate the Bible but also to interpret it. The New English Bible is a signal example of this. Too often the NEB translators in their desire to interpret the text give what is more like a paraphrase than a translation. When in the NEB at Matthew 5.3 we read 'How blest are those who know their need of God!', we may well wonder what has happened to the literal sense 'Blessed are the poor in spirit'. The NEB translators are not content to translate the sentence; they want at the same time to explain what it means, or what they think it means. Another instance occurs in the NEB rendering of Isaiah 53.11a. The NEB offers: 'After all his pains he shall be bathed in light.' This translation is based on a reconstruction of the Hebrew. In the extant Hebrew text there is no word meaning 'bathed' and no word meaning 'light'. The translation 'bathed in light' is in fact a conjectural restoration of the Hebrew text inspired by the Greek, where the word 'light' appears. The translators have not even had the grace to append a note telling us that this is a conjectural restoration of the original text. So if you are studying the Bible in detail, do not confine yourself to one translation only.

From one point of view it might be claimed that with the advent of biblical criticism Protestantism has lost its *raison d'être*. All the reformed churches that broke away from the mediaeval church in the sixteenth century justified their action by appealing to the Bible against what was then held to be the tradition of the church. But now at the end of the twentieth century, thanks largely to the labours of Protestant scholars, the Bible could be said to have fallen to pieces in our hands. If we are honest we must admit that it is neither inerrant, nor inspired, nor internally consistent in all its parts. Most of the presuppositions according to which the church has always interpreted the Bible have proved to be mistaken. But such a conclusion would be wrong. If we have succeeded in showing in this book that the Bible is neither exploded, nor discredited, nor rendered useless, but that on the contrary, it is still the essential foundation on which the church's faith rests and that it can still be a source of hope and inspiration to Christians, then the intention with which we set out to write this work will have been amply fulfilled.

Suggestions for Further Reading

Interpretation of the Bible

Alan Richardson and T. W. Schweitzer (eds), *Biblical Authority for Today*, SCM Press 1951.

Alan Richardson, 'The Rise of Modern Biblical Scholarship and Recent Discussion of the Authority of the Bible' in S. L. Greenslade (ed.), *The Cambridge History of the Bible*, vol. 2, Cambridge University Press 1963.

Michael Green, *The Authority of Scripture*, Falcon 1963.

Stephen Neill, *The Interpretation of the New Testament 1861–1961*, Oxford University Press 1964 (second updated edition to 1986, with T. Wright, 1988).

Dennis Nineham, *The Use and Abuse of the Bible*, Macmillan 1976.

Stephen Neill's book is an admirably clear account of the impact of biblical criticism on the study of the New Testament. Nineham has some valuable comments to make, but leaves one with little to hold on to.

Inspiration

J. Burnaby, *Is the Bible Inspired?*, Duckworth 1949.

J. T. Burtchaell, *Catholic Theories of Biblical Inspiration since 1810*, Cambridge University Press 1969.

B. Vawter, *Biblical Inspiration*, Hutchinson and Westminster Press 1972.

P. J. Achtemeier, *The Inspiration of Scripture*, Westminster Press 1980.

All these books tackle the central question of how you can describe a not-infallible book as inspired and show various answers have been given.

Fundamentalism

B. B. Warfield, *The Inspiration and Authority of the Bible*, second edition, Marshall, Morgan & Scott 1951.

J. K. S. Reid, *The Authority of Scripture*, Methuen 1957.

J. I. Packer, *Fundamentalism and the Word of God*, Inter-Varsity Press 1958.

R. K. Harrison, *Introduction to the Old Testament*, Inter-Varsity Press 1970.

R. K. Harrison, *Old Testament Times*, Inter-Varsity Press 1970.

Hans Küng and J. Moltmann, 'The Fundamental Understanding of Scripture', in *Concilium*, 1980, pp. 70–74.

James Barr, *Fundamentalism*, SCM Press and Westminster Press 1981.

James Barr, *Escaping from Fundamentalism*, SCM Press 1984 (= *Beyond Fundamentalism*, Westminster Press 1984).

N. M. S. Cameron, *Biblical Higher Criticism and the Defense of Infallibilism in Nineteenth Century Britain*, E. Mellen 1987.

R. K. Harrison's books are included as an example of how a fundamentalist scholar deals with the Old Testament. Reid's book is an attempt to show that the great Reformers were not fundamentalists in the modern sense. James Barr tries to convert the fundamentalist by beginning from an inside knowledge of his mentality.

The Development of Doctrine

R. P. C. Hanson, *The Attractiveness of God*, SPCK 1973, ch. 2.
A. T. Hanson and R. P. C. Hanson, *Reasonable Belief*, Oxford University Press 1980, pp. 189–195.
R. P. C. Hanson, *The Continuity of Christian Doctrine*, Seabury Press 1981.

Richard Hanson was an expert on the early Fathers and has consequently devoted much thought to the question of the development of doctrine.

The Canon

A. Souter, *Text and Canon in the New Testament*, Duckworth 1954.
F. V. Filson, *Which Books Belong to the Bible?*, Westminster Press 1957.
James Barr, *Holy Scripture: Canon, Authority, Criticism*, Oxford University Press 1983.
F. F. Bruce, *The Canon of Scripture*, Chapter House 1988.

Souter's book is a well-known text-book on the subject. Bruce's work is very recent and gives an able presentation of the facts about the canon.

Index of Biblical and Other References

Index of Names